One Minute Messages

An anthology of "old popular" and "new original"
thoughts, stories, poetry and prose.

**by
Dan Clark
with
Michael Gale**

Sunrise Publishing

Second Printing, 1990

Third Printing, 1992

Library of Congress Catalog number 86-82476
ISBN 0-916095-13-4

Acknowledgements

True leadership comes from inspirational communicators; those select individuals who possess the ability to move others into action; those rare men and women of history who practice a belief in the words of Zig Ziglar: "You can get everything in life you want, if you help enough other people get what they want."

This work is dedicated to the quiet heroes and great motivational teachers, comedians and storytellers who have influenced our lives: Napolean Hill, Earl Nightingale, Dr. Norman Vincent Peale, Zig Ziglar, Dr. Robert Schuller, Paul Dunn, Bill Cosby, David Brenner, Mr. and Mrs. S. Wayne Clark, Dr. and Mrs. Donald Gale, Kelly (K.C. Clark) and our many friends, teachers, and relatives who cared enough to not just "talk the talk" – but "walk the walk" of example.

Special thanks to Stan and Sharon Miller for their permission to use any materials found in their publications.

Table of Contents

A Sense of Purpose
Leaders Help Those Around Them
Leaders Know Words Rule The World

Treat Her Like A Lady
Girls, What Are You Advertising?
The Plea — By A Girl
Answer To The Plea — By A Boy

You Get What You Look For
Don't Shun Competition
Competition Brings Out Our Best
Today
Idleness Breeds Fatigue
The Hope Of The Future
A Banner Year
No Free Lunches Anymore
Self-Motivation: The One That Really Works
Your Hometown
The Key
The Secret of Getting Rich
Opportunity Exists in America
The Modern Little Red Hen
Where Did The Money Go?
The Promise of America
Are You Lucky?
Everybody's Favorite Subject
Give It A Try
It Can Be Done
Liberty

The Control of Champions
The Desk That Moved
Watch Out
Making Things Happen
Responsibility In All Areas of Life
How Much Freedom Is Too Much?
You Only Hurt Yourself
A Police Car In The Mirror

Become Enthusiastic
Give Yourself Another Chance
Keep On Shooting

Turn Your Lemons Into Lemonade
How Hard Do You Push Yourself?
Don't Feel Inferior
The Worst Usually Never Happens
You Can't Buy Happiness, But You Can Find It
Face Problems Don't Run From Them
Dealing With Fear
Do The Worst Part First
Dealing With Problems
Champions Don't Feel Pressure

Only Perfect Practice Makes Perfect
Demographic Portrait of America
Getting By Lately?
Learning Is Not An 8 To 5 Job
What Is Involved Evolves
Great Teachers Can Find Hidden Potential
The State of Becoming
Learn It Now; Apply It Later
Books
Learn It Now
How To Pass Class

Look Hard Before You Leave Home
I Don't Know What To Do
Growing Up Is Tough
Its Not A Way Out
I Never Thought They'd Do It

They Ought To Rent Beer Not Sell It
A Word of Wisdom
Drunk-Driving is Everyone's Business
An Eye Opener
The Dumb Things We Do When We Drive
Drinking Is Scary
Some Things Never Change
Don't Do It

Be Not Weary
Count The Windows In Your World

The Best Way To Play Any Game

The Challenge

"Life is a tough teacher — it gives the test first and then the lesson afterward."

We hope you learn from our hindsight, mistakes, successes, philosophies, observations, and favorite quotes, jokes and stories that you may understand some lessons from life. We want to help you effectively study for your daily exams in the school of hard knocks.

As you read, we challenge you to take time to pause and ponder and realize what is happening to you. Remember, "Man's mind once stretched by a new idea, never regains its original dimensions."

Preface Insight
— *by Michael Gale*

We have a lot coming at us in today's world. A lot of society's worst products are being marketed directly at young and old: Drugs, MTV, fad clothes, tasteless movies, and cosmetics guaranteeing to make us more beautiful and popular are targeted directly at each of us every day. And behind this sales campaign are some of the brightest, most persuasive minds in our country. They are making millions creating these needs in the minds of the consumer. The truth is, some of the things being popularized and making some rich probably aren't doing the rest of us a bit of good.

Somehow, someone, in the midst of this media mind-bombardment should remind us there are a few basic things we should remember in order to achieve a happy, successful life. For example, students, learning to use their minds, should be taught how to channel those powerful minds in a positive direction, a direction that promises success. As young adults seeking to gain control of their lives, they should be told about the problems drugs, breaking the law, or unwanted pregnancies have caused other students their age.

Most importantly, even more important than the warnings and consequences of bad behavior, young people as well as older adults should be taught they are important. We should be taught that we make a significant difference, that each of us was born to succeed and can succeed. We need to be taught how to be champions and feel like champions. We need to know how to overcome the fear we all have of not wanting to try for fear of failure. We need to be motivated and learn how to believe in ourselves.

That's a tall order for any book to try and accomplish, but Dan and I wanted to give it a try. We wanted to write a book selling qualities, truths and values we all need to learn in order to become successful, happy people. You see, Dan and I went through those crazy years of youthful and young adult development together and we were lucky; we had coaches, parents and leaders around us to inspire and motivate us. That's why we wanted to pass it on to you. We feel these "one minute messages" can give that motivation and inspiration to anyone who reads them. Some of the messages are humorous, some are philosophical, some heart-warming, while others concentrate on famous people and what they overcame to get where they wanted to go. Some are directed specifically to young people — all have an important message for everyone.

Helping Dan Clark write this book changed my mind set in a lot of ways. I felt a steaming positiveness take hold of me as I edited each message and helped it come to life on the page. I really did start to believe anything is possible if we set our minds to it. I have only one regret about the book. It's a shame those who read it may not have the benefit of hearing each message personally from Dan Clark, because Dan's delivery and personality are unforgettable and have gained him notoriety across the country. You'll miss his flare for drama and his lively sense of humor. If you ever get a chance to hear Dan in person, seize it. While you're waiting, enjoy what this book has to say and teach. I like what helping write it did to me.

Michael Gale

Humor, Quotes, and Communication
An Introduction

— by Dan Clark

When the publishers were trying to find someone to write this book, they called up the best looking guy they knew. He turned them down. So they called up the most intelligent guy they knew. He turned them down too. So they called up the most humble, sweetest, most sincere, serious guy they knew. Hey, I couldn't turn them down three times in a row, so I said yes!

Obviously this book is conceived out of the notion that we should laugh – and also that we should take time each day to smile, think, feel, and perhaps even cry. It's therapeutic and important to our mental health. We need to take time to be stimulated and motivated to smell the roses! And this stimulus doesn't have to come in an elaborate wordy way. For example, when it comes to explanations, sometimes I feel like a mosquito in a nudest colony – I don't know where to start. So, I just relate basic statements and pray: "Please make my words all soft and sweet, I don't know which I'll have to eat." As a matter of fact, each of us will be much better off if we always cut through the babbling rhetoric and stick to simple straightforward statements and principles of practical use. Remember, we act like we think and talk. I'm sure you'll agree as you analyze individuals around you; there sure are a lot of mighty interesting, complicated, spacey folks out there! I stopped a man in a hotel one day to ask how to get to the ballroom and he gave me accurate, precise directions, and then ended with a meaningful poem.

I'm scared! I don't know whether the world is full of smart men bluffing or imbeciles who mean it! Some people should realize the world is a black tuxedo and they're a pair of brown shoes! Am I being critical? Yes, because some people are not being authentically themselves. Perhaps I don't have room to talk; I had some challenges growing up. In fact, sometimes I think, "If I could get myself in position, I'd give myself a kick in the rear!" A lot of us cover up who we really are and try to be too complicated and too cool; we try to be too open-minded.

Samuel Butler said, "An open mind is all very well in its way, but it ought not to be so open that there is no keeping anything in or out of it. It should be capable of shutting its doors sometimes, or it may be found a little drafty." Think about it — I know you know a few people who when they walk by, you hear the ocean in their ears. My best friend is a great guy - but let's face it, he's just not wrapped too tight! I swear his butter has just plumb slipped off his bisquit!!

This is why I stress this point. We should shed our facades and strive to be intelligent, practical and basic by looking for the simple truths in life. George Bernard Shaw wrote, "Common sense is instinct — enough of it is genius." Let us therefore experience the wisdom in learning simple, short mental meals. I have screened and compiled a list of some of my favorites. They are in a specific order to take you from hello to goodbye on the road to developing a positive mental attitude. They prove true the statement by Robert Assagioli: "The power of words — of great thoughts to quicken and motivate one's life, is immeasurable."

Quips & Quotations

"A man who talks by the yard and thinks by the inch, needs to be kicked by the foot."

"If at first you do succeed, try to hide your astonishment."

"If at first you don't succeed, you're about average."

"Always do right. This will gratify some people and astonish the rest." — *Mark Twain*

"Most smiles are started by another smile."

"The greatest artist was once a beginner."

"Don't be the guy who has a big hat and no cattle. Do more than talk the talk — walk the walk!"

"Seek constantly new resources — the mind and spirit must have their thirst satisfied."

"It's easy to be brave at a safe distance. To see what is right and not to do it, is want of courage." — *Aesop*

"You've got to be willing to go out on a limb — that's where the fruit is!"

"Do your best this hour and you will be better the next."

"Commandment number one of any truly civilized society: Let people be different." — *David Grayson*

"No race of people can prosper until it learns that there is as much dignity in tilling a field as in writing a poem." — *Booker T. Washington*

"In striving for perfection, one attains excellence, not perfection."

"Today I gave everything that I had to give, because anything I saved has been wasted." — *S. Wayne Clark*

"As long as man imagines that he cannot do a certain thing, he is correct and it is impossible for him to do it." — *Spinoza*

"Without doubt the most common weakness of all human beings is the habit of leaving their minds open to the negative influence of other people." — *Napoleon Hill*

"There is a field for critics, no doubt, but we don't remember seeing statues of any of them in the Hall of Fame."

"Believe that you possess significant reserves of health, energy, and endurance, and your belief will create the fact." — *William James*

"You cannot run away from a weakness; you must sometime fight it out or perish; and if that be so, why not now, and where you stand?" — *Robert Louis Stevenson*

"For they had learned that true safety was to be found in long previous training and not in eloquent exhortations uttered when they were going into action." — *Thucydides*

"The difference between peak performers and everybody else is much smaller than everybody else thinks. More encouragingly, the special qualities present in high achievers are learnable; they are not reserved for only a lucky few who have been blessed by genetic good fortune. Anyone can succeed if they are willing to work hard enough." — *Charles Garfield*

"The more you practice what you know, the more you'll know what to practice." —*Tom Gadd*

Did you extract some meaningful messages from these simple statements? Can you see the value of digging through the tons of wordy dirt just to find the nuggets of precious golden truth? One short precious concept, thought, or story could be the very catalyst that changes your life for the best. Mark Van Doren reminds us, "Bring ideas in and entertain each of them royally, for one of them may be the king."

For this reason I would like to introduce an idea and entertain it:

"The Necessity of Humor and Effective Communication"

Goethe wrote, "Men show their character in nothing more clearly than by what they think laughable." I agree! Developing a sense of humor is a key to success. We need to learn to laugh at others (when appropriate), with others, and especially at ourselves!

Humor

Why do we take ourselves so seriously? Who says we can't look at the bright side of everything and find humor in all we do? The truth is we can, we should, we must in order to survive! Humor is therapeutic and an essential part to good mental health. Let me prove it in the following real life situations and classic "old jokes."

Golf is a funny game! My friend, Todd, is so bad he usually waits until he hits his first drive before he knows which course he's playing that day. I'm not going to say he's unpredictable off the tee, but Todd is the first person I know to make golf a contact sport. And does he ever lose balls? Usually about twelve by the third hole! One day, Todd even lost three balls in the ball washer!!

Baseball is another amusing game. One summer I worked part time as a Babe Ruth League baseball umpire. During one game, Randy O'Brien, the fastest pitcher in the league, was on the mound. He was so fast he could have thrown a strawberry through a battleship! A young player came up to bat. Nervously, he dug in and prepared to hit. O'Brien rared back and threw a speeding fast ball down the middle.

I yelled out "Strike One." The young batter turned around and whined, "C'mon ump. That wasn't a strike." I asked, "Why, did you see it?" He answered, "No, but it sounded high!"

Football coaches are even amusing! I guess they have to be! Without a sense of humor they couldn't survive. For example, when Houston Oilers Football Coach, John Breen, was asked why his team lost the game, he answered "We were tipping off our plays. Whenever we broke from the huddle, the opposing team knew who was going to carry the ball. Three of the backs were laughing and one was pale as a ghost!"

How about football players? A naive, Georgia high school football player received a phone call from the coach at the University of Tennessee. The coach asked the player to come to the school for a recruiting visit. The boy went to the Atlanta airport and inquired, "I want to go from Atlanta to Knoxville, Tennessee. What time does the plane take off and get there?" The ticket lady answered, "The plane takes off at 4:00 p.m. and gets to Tennessee at 3:45 p.m. Would you like to buy a ticket?" Not understanding the time zone change, the big eyed astonished boy replied, "No, I don't want a ticket. But I sure would like to watch the plane take off!"

It's true. People constantly say funny things:

One day a man came up to me and asked, "Why do you speak for a living? Why do you need all this attention? Are you insecure?" I started to think, "Yes, I guess I am insecure. My whole life I've wondered whether or not I was adopted." So, after all these years of insecurity and wonderment, I finally got up enough courage to ask my father if I was adopted. I walked into his room and said, "Ling Chow — am I adopted?" (If you don't get it, look at my picture on the back cover of the book.)

One day I was waiting in a hotel lobby. I was sitting on a bench and sitting on a folded newspaper. As I sat there on the newspaper, a man walked up to me and asked, "Excuse me sir, are you reading that?" About an hour later the exact same thing happened, but this time I was prepared. As I sat there on the newspaper, a man asked, "Excuse me, are you reading that?" I stood up, turned the page, sat back down, and answered, "Yes, but I'll be done in a minute!"

Even food sometimes forces us to laugh. At my house the food is so bad we pray after we eat! And when I go out to eat, the laughter continues:

One day I was sitting in a restaurant and the man sitting next to me asked the waitress what the special of the day was. She replied, "Cows Tongue." In response, the man said, "Yuck, how could anyone eat anything that had been in something's mouth. Would you please bring me 2 eggs."

One day a naive country boy was visiting the big city for the first time. Entering an office building, he saw an overweight older woman step into an elevator — something he'd never seen before. Suddenly the doors slid together and closed, little lighted numbers flashed, the doors slid open, and a beautiful young model stepped out. Blinking in amazement, the country boy scratched his head and drawled, "Shoulda brought mah wife!"

I have also observed that mothers have brain damage! Mothers say funny things, like, "Don't climb up in that tree. If you fall down and break both your legs, don't you dare come running to me!" How about when I asked my mother to help me, even though she was busy in the kitchen? She replied, "I only have two hands!" I was afraid to look at other moms! What did they have, nine hands?

Children also say funny things. I overheard a thirteen-year-old say to his dad, "I'm starting to like girls, and I hate it!"

My friend's three-year-old son found his father's military identification tag and asked his mother, "What's this, Mommy?" "That's your father's dog tag," she replied. He promptly asked, "When was Daddy a dog?"

My brother's wife was pregnant with her third baby at the same time my neighbor's dog was about to have her pups. Thinking that now would be the perfect time to explain how babies come into the world, my brother brought his two children to see the birth of the seven puppies. Months later, when my brother's wife had her baby, we were all at the hospital standing at the nursery window. My brother's three-year-old son looked at the rows of babies, all asleep, and asked, "Are these all ours?"

We can even laugh about testing situations:

A soldier was working in the base warehouse when a phone call came in requesting an inventory check. The soldier replied, "We have ten tanks, twenty rifles, and one fat headed sergeant's jeep." The man on the other end angrily countered, "Do you know who this is?" The soldier replied, "No." The caller said, "This is the sergeant!" The soldier swallowed hard and countered, "Do you know who this is?" The sergeant answered, "No." The soldier replied, "Good, Bye Bye Fat Head."

A man was sitting in a restaurant when two big men walked in. They walked straight up to the man and beat him up, knocking him unconscious, and left him on the floor. As they were leaving, the two men explained to the doorman, "When he wakes up, tell him that was Karáte from Korea and Judo from Japan." The assaulted man finally woke up and left the restaurant. An hour later, the two big men came back in to eat. Moments later, the man they beat up returned and walked straight up to their table. He promptly beat both men up and left them unconscious on the floor. As he left the restaurant, he explained to the doorman, "When they wake up, tell them that was a crowbar from Sears!"

A lady had been married four different times. First to a banker, again to an entertainer, again to a preacher, and last to a funeral director. When asked why, the lady replied, "One for the money, two for the show, three to get ready, and four to go!"

You see, we can laugh! We can find humor in every-thing — in ourselves, in relationships, in children, and even in religion.

A man went to confess his sins. In the confessional he admitted that for years he had been stealing building supplies from the woodshop where he worked. "What did you take?" the priest asked. "Enough to build my house and three mountain cottages." "This is very serious," the priest said. "I'll have to give you a stiff penance. Have you ever done a retreat?" "No, Father, I haven't," the man replied. "But if you can get the plans, I can get the lumber!"

Two nuns were driving in their car when they ran out of gas. They walked two miles to a country house to find some help. The farmer gave them some gas, and asked the nuns, "Is it okay if I put the gas in this bedpan? I don't have a gas can for you to carry it in." The nuns didn't mind, thanked the farmer, and walked the two miles back to their car. One nun held the gas tank open while the other nun poured the gas from the bedpan. Just then a Protestant minister drove by. Seeing what was going on, he stopped, rolled down his window, and said, "Excuse me sisters. I'm not of your religion, but I couldn't help admiring your faith!"

When I was playing football, before every game the coach would call on a player to offer the pre-game prayer. On one occasion with everyone excited and psyched up to play ball, the praying player suddenly stopped in the middle of the prayer. Dead silence filled the room which seemed to last for eternity. Finally, a guy on the back row yelled out, "Amen." The praying player answered, "Thanks man, I've been trying to think of that word for five minutes!"

11

We could go on and on, so let's do! But let's shift gears to communication and look at it in several ways.

Communication

Communication is an exact science, involving two or more persons, that can be separated into two parts — the sender of the message and the receiver of the message. If there is a discrepancy between the sender's message and the receiver's understanding, there is a failure to communicate.

This failure is one of the biggest problems facing our society today. In the family, there isn't a generation gap, there is a communication gap. In business, there isn't a management/employee or productivity problem, it's usually a communication problem.

Failure to communicate can also be humorous. Take the example of the water closet:

The Water Closet

An English lady was looking for some rooms to rent in Switzerland and asked the local village schoolmaster to help her. A place that suited her was finally found and the lady returned to London for her belongings. She remembered that she had not noticed a bathroom, or as she called it, a water closet, so she wrote to the schoolmaster. He was puzzled by the initials "W.C.," never dreaming, of course, that she was asking about a bathroom. He finally asked the parish priest who decided that W.C. stood for Westbrook Church. This was his reply:

Dear Madam,

The W.C. is situated nine miles from the house in the center of a beautiful grove of trees. It is capable of holding 350 people at a time and is open on Tuesday, Thursday, and Sunday each week. A large number of folks attend during the summer months, so it is suggested you go early, although there is plenty of standing room. Some folks like to take their lunch and make a day of it, especially on Thursday when there is organ accompaniment.

It may be of interest to you to know that my daughter met her husband in our W.C. and was also married there.

We hope you will be there in time for our bazaar to be held very soon. The proceeds will go toward the purchase of plush seats which the folks agree are a long-felt need, as the present seats all have holes in them.

I shall close now with the desire to accommodate you in every way possible and I will be happy to save you a seat down front or near the door, whichever you prefer.

Sincerely,
Schoolmaster

More Mixups

Communication isn't just fouled up through misunderstanding. It also fails when the sender of the message doesn't say what he means to say. The following are genuine examples of notes that teachers received from home:

1. Dear School, please excuse John from being absent on January 29, 30, 31, 32, 33, and also 34.
2. Please excuse Jimmy for being. It was his father's fault.
3. John has been absent because he had two teeth taken off his face.
4. My son has been under the doctor's care and should not take fizecal ed. Please execute him.
5. My daughter was absent yesterday because she was tired. She spent the weekend with the Marines.
6. Mary Ann was absent Dec. 11-16 because she had a

fever, sore throat, headache, and upset stomach. Her sister was also sick, fever and sore throat, her brother had a low grade fever and ached all over. I wasn't feeling the best either, sore throat and fever. There must be a flu going around, her father even got hot last night.

7. Please excuse Sara for being absent. She was sick and I had her shot.

8. It wasn't Jimmy's fault that he doesn't have his homework. The dog ate it. It was hard. We had to force him to do it, but he did it.

Communication also involves interpretation. Therefore, to effectively communicate, we need to agree on the definition of what communication is. Something to one may be different to another. For example, what is good music? Beethoven or Twisted Sister? I overheard a father talking about his children. He said, "My kids love a form of music called 'heavy metal.' I'm not completely sure of this but I think it's called 'heavy metal' because the lead singer usually sounds like he's dropped an anvil on his foot!"

Learning to laugh and take ourselves less seriously is essential to successful living. Learning to be serious and responsible is also a key to joy and self fulfillment. Therefore, learning to effectively understand, interpret, and thus communicate is of utmost importance!

So, I close this introduction in hopes that you will accept my desire to communicate my thoughts and feelings to you through the following "One Minute Messages." They are a collection of one page "mental meals" to be read each day for the first half year. Then start again and re-read them for the second half year. They are designed to help you positively approach the way you attack school, work, and play.

I realize positive thinking doesn't guarantee success, but is sure does increase possibilities for it. And when you realize the benefits and intricate details of how it works, you too will understand why positive thinking works with

14

some individuals and not with others. Simply: you cannot perform consistently in a manner that is inconsistent with the way you see yourself performing and living. Therefore, the purpose of this book is to help you develop a habit of positive thought at the start of each day. This will help you sustain positive thinking throughout the week, month, and year, and assist you to be consistent in your optomistic outlook on living.

I have co-authored this book with my long time friend, Michael Gale, for a specific reason. He is a very sensitive, successful man who is aware of current beneficial issues. We grew up together and experienced ups and downs that truly taught us "principles in practice from the school of hard knocks." That's why we teamed up to compile this work. We believe the following favorite stories and personal philosophies will help you succeed. It is our hope that you will not only use them as psychological shots in your arm, but that you will share them with others in the many presentations you may be asked to give along your way. And as you do, I leave you with one final challenge, to share:

I challenge you to Drink, Swear, Steal and Lie!

* Drink — from the fountain of love and friendship found in mankind;

* Swear — that today will be the best day of the rest of your life;

* Steal — a little extra time to do something special for someone when you know you won't get the credit;

* Lie — when you lie down at night, thank the God above that you live in the greatest country in the world! Happy Trails!

Dan Clark

15

"ONE MINUTE MESSAGES"

To divide this section from the humorous beginning and to appropriately introduce these "ONE MINUTE MESSAGES," Michael and I decided to shock you. We relate this first true story in hopes that you will feel the impact and far reaching message that can come from a one page essay. We truly want to change your life and begin the "messages" with the following foundation category:

LOVE AND FRIENDSHIP

Pause and Patiently Ponder

How many times do we fail to realize the difference between the person and the performance – the difference between who we are and what we do? Just because we make mistakes doesn't make us stupid individuals. We're only human – we're supposed to make mistakes!

A man came out of his home to once again admire the new truck he had purchased the day before. To his bewilderment, his three-year-old son was happily hammering dents into it's shiny paint job. The man "flew off the handle," ran to his son, knocked him away, and to punish him, hammered the little boy's little hands, beating them to a pulp.

The father finally calmed down enough to take his son to the hospital. The doctor operated, trying desperately to save the crushed bones, but had to amputate the little boy's fingers from both hands.

The next morning when his son woke up from surgery and noticed his stubs, he politely and innocently said, "Daddy, I'm sorry about your truck, but when are my fingers going to grow back?"

The father went home and committed suicide.

Think about this story the next time you see someone spill milk at the dinner table, or hear a baby cry at night for food or a diaper change, or lose your patience with someone you should love and care for. Remember, trucks can be repaired — sometimes people and their feelings can't! Pause and ponder. Think before you act. Be patient, understand, and love!

A Brother Like That

Paul received a new automobile from his brother as a birthday present. When Paul came out of his office, a young boy asked, "Is this your car mister?" Paul nodded, "My brother gave it to me for my birthday." The boy looked astounded. "You mean your brother gave it to you, and it didn't cost you nothing? Gosh, I wish . . ." He hesitated, and Paul knew what he was going to wish. He was going to wish he had a brother like that. But what the lad said jarred Paul. "I wish," the boy went on, "that I could be a brother like that."

Paul looked at the boy in astonishment, then impulsively he added, "Would you like a ride in my car?" "Oh, yes, I'd love that!" After a short ride the boy turned, and with his eyes aglow said, "Mister, would you mind riding in front of my house?" Paul smiled a little. He thought he knew what the lad wanted. He wanted to show his neighbors that he could ride in a big automobile. But Paul was wrong again.

"Will you stop right where those steps are?" the boy asked. He ran up the steps and came out carrying his little polio-crippled brother. He sat him down on the bottom step and pointed to the car. "There she is Buddy, just like I told you upstairs. His brother gave it to him for his birthday and someday I'm going to give you one just like it; then you can see for yourself all the pretty things in the store windows that I've been trying to tell you about."

Paul got out and lifted the little lad to the front seat of his car, and the three of them began a memorable ride. That night Paul learned the true definition of: IT IS MORE BLESSED TO GIVE . . . .

Tell Them Today

Do you ever have bad days when you want to scream at everyone, even those you care about? One girl did.

She'd had a terrible day at school and was behind in her studies. When she got home from school, her little brother and his friend were playing with her lipstick. "Stay out of my stuff, you little pest," she screamed.

Her brother's face turned red, and he apologized, but the girl didn't let up. She ignored him during dinner and even the next morning as she got ready for school. He begged her not to be mad at him and to forgive him. But still she decided to hold her grudge and make him pay, thinking she would accept his apology that afternoon.

But when she came home from school, it was too late. Her brother's badly twisted bike was on the lawn. Her mother and father were sitting in the front room crying. There on the ground with a sheet over his head was her baby brother. Timmy was dead.

Her remorse was magnified as she grabbed his lifeless body and begged him to be alive. But it was too late. She thought of all the reasons she loved him, and she wished she could take him in her arms and say, "I love you; of course I forgive you." But it was too late.

Don't wait until it's too late to tell the people you love how you feel about them. Don't be caught saying, "If only." Love today! Try to catch someone doing something right!

Say Something Nice

It isn't hard to say something nice about someone.

A young couple had a baby who was physically perfect except for one thing: He was born with no ears. The parents of this young baby were extremely worried about how difficult life would be for their child. They feared the ridicule he would undergo from other kids when he got older and had to go to school. They wanted to introduce their son to other children before that dreaded day to see what the reaction would be. They asked one of their neighbors to bring over their little girls to the house.

Instead of showing up with their daughters, the neighbors showed up with their eight-year-old son who was known for his mean mouth. If you had bad breath he wouldn't just say it, he would fall to the floor and faint.

Full of reservations, they introduced their son to the little boy and waited for a reaction. He looked at him lying in the bed. Finally the mean little boy asked, "Are his eyes good?"

"Well, yes. Why?" asked the concerned parents.

"Because he's going to have a hard time wearing glasses."

Even the most obnoxious person doesn't have to say something mean. Don't notice everything wrong with people. Notice what they have going for them. If you look a little closer than first appearances you'll find the rose instead of the thorn.

The Last Game

Let's say it was the last football game of your senior year, and a message came that your father had died. That's what happened to John. Just before the game, the coach told John, knowing he would elect not to play. But instead of reacting strongly, John just took it all in stride and said, "I'll go right after the game."

The coach knew John spoke highly of his father and expected him to grieve. When he didn't, the coach said, "Hey you don't have to play; the game isn't that important."

John ignored him and played anyway. John was the star. He helped win the game pretty much on his own. He played possessed. It was as if he had been let out of a cage.

After the game, other players offered condolences but were appauled at John's lack of concern. John was casual and happy. The coach was mad and thought he had taught John too much dedication for sports and not enough compassion. He asked John: "Why did you play the game, John? Your father is dead. I'm ashamed I let you play. I'm ashamed of you."

John replied, "Coach, this is our last game. I am a senior. I love my dad and this was the first time my dad has ever seen me play, and I had to play like I never played before."

"But your father's dead," the coach replied.

John choked up. With tears streaming down his cheeks, he smiled at the coach. "You didn't know my father was blind, did you?"

It's What's On The Inside

For all the different kinds and colors of people in the world, there still is one thing we have in common.

On a spring day in New York's Central Park, a balloon salesman was busy trying to sell his balloons to passersby. In order to gain the attention of those walking in the park, from time to time he would release a brightly colored balloon and let it rise into the sky.

As he worked this sunny afternoon, a little black girl approached him. She was shy and had a poor self-image. She had been watching the man and had a question for him.

"Mister if you let a black balloon go, will it rise, too?" The balloon salesman knew what the girl was asking.

"Sweetheart," he explained. "It doesn't matter what color the balloon is. It's not what's on the outside that makes it rise, it's what's on the inside that makes it go up."

People are people! There is no superior race or color. Look at people like the many flavors of ice cream. If the heat is on, we're all going to melt. If we get the cold shoulder we freeze up. The ingredients are the same; only the colors are different. Bigotry and racism only cause hate and ruin what's inside of you. As you meet people; overlook the cover and color of the book, and take time to open the pages. We were born to live and let live and love!

Think Before You Act

An Alaskan trapper lost his wife and was left with a two-year-old daughter. At times he had to leave the little girl with his faithful dog so he could work in the woods. While away during such an absence one afternoon, a terrible blizzard came up. The trapper was forced to take refuge in a hollow tree to save his life. At daybreak he rushed to his cabin. The door was open. His dog, covered with blood, looked at him from the corner of his eye. The father's blood froze in his veins. Just one thing had happened he was sure — his dog had turned wolf and killed his child. He reached for his ax and in a moment he buried it in the skull of the dog he had trusted.

Like a maniac he scanned the scene. In desperation he uncovered the remnants of his cabin. The furniture was cracked and tipped over from the battle which had taken place. Suddenly a faint cry came from under the bed. His daughter was hiding under it safe and sound. He hugged his daughter. Looking further he saw the bloody remains of a wolf in the corner. Then he knew his dog had saved his child from the fierce fangs of the wolf.

With just a brief moment of caution the trapper could have held both his child and the dog in his arms, instead, there was remorse. Don't act hastily. Weigh all things before you strike.

We can't afford to pre-judge and label situations or people. We need to love, listen, learn and then evaluate and act.

Forgive The Mistakes Of Others

Tom was nervous as he sat on the train and the old man sitting next to him sensed this.

"Son, what's the matter with you?"

"I just got out of prison," replied the young man named Tom. My mistake broke my parents' hearts and caused them a lot of shame. I still love them but I don't know if they really love me after what I did. I never let them visit me in prison. I told them they didn't have to let me come home if they were too ashamed of me. I live in a small town with a large tree by the railroad tracks. I told them to tie a ribbon around that ol' tree if they were willing to let me get off." Tom paused as the old man listened, then continued.

"The reason I'm so nervous is that we're almost there and I'm scared to look at that tree. I feel I don't deserve my parents because I hurt them so much."

Tom choked up and looked down in shame. Neither man spoke as the train slowed down to come to a stop at the next station; it was Tom's home town. Tom couldn't look, it was the old man who nudged him and said, "I think you can look now, son."

Tom looked up slowly. The old tree was covered with hundreds of ribbons — red ones, blue ones, yellow, orange and green. Tom turned to the old man with tears in his eyes and said, "They still love me. I'll see you mister, I'm going home."

Love Is A Miracle

We can all be vehicles for loving another person. Likewise, other persons can be vehicles for loving us. Every day there are opportunities to give and receive love. This story might explain what I mean.

One cold evening during the holiday season a little boy about six or seven was standing out in front of a store window. The little child had no shoes and his clothes were mere rags. A young woman passing by saw the little boy and could read the longing in his pale blue eyes. She took the child by the hand and led him into the store. There she bought him some new shoes and a complete suit of warm clothing. They came back outside into the street and the woman said to the child, "Now you can go home and have a very happy holiday."

The little boy looked up at her and asked, "Are you God, Ma'am?"

She smiled down at him and replied, "No son, I'm just one of his children."

The little boy then said, "I knew you had to be some relation."

Love is a miracle! It can come to any of us at any age, at any time, and in any place. All we have to do is reach out and live, reach out and give, reach out and receive. Love works!

A Loving Brother

As the screeching of car brakes subsided, ten-year-old Eddie pulled himself to his feet, and screamed his little sister's name whose hand he had been holding.

Eddie's screams brought no reply. Eddie limped over to a crowd of men gathered around a car just in time to hear a policeman say, "She's got a pulse, she might live."

Everything was kind of a blur to Eddie. Ambulances came and took them both to the hospital. Eddie responded to questions from some men about his parents. Eddie's father was dead and his mother worked, he didn't know where.

At the hospital one of the doctors said to Eddie, "Your sister is bleeding internally. We'll need a transfusion of your blood for her to live. Will you do it for her?"

Eddie grew pale and gripped the chair he was sitting on tightly, then nodded his head as he gulped. The doctor took Eddie into the operating room with his little sister and ran a plastic line from her arm to his.

"How long before I die?" asked Eddie.

"What do you mean," asked the surgeon.

"Well, when a guy gives away his blood he dies doesn't he?" replied Eddie. At that moment the doctors and nurses realized what a sacrifice young Eddie was ready to make for his sister. Tears filled their eyes, and the surgeon hugged Eddie and told him he would be okay. His sister Agnes, too. And that day they all learned about true selfless love.

Serve!

One night, at 11:30 p.m., an older black lady was standing on the side of an Alabama highway trying to endure a lashing rain storm. Her car had broken down and she desperately needed a ride. Soaking wet, she decided to flag down the next car. A young white man stopped to help her — generally unheard of in the deep south during the conflict-filled 1960's. The man took her to safety, helped her get assistance and put her into a taxi cab. She seemed to be in a big hurry! She wrote down his address, thanked him and drove away.

Seven days went by and a knock came on the man's door. To his surprise, a giant combination console color TV and stereo record player was delivered to his home. A special note was attached. The note read:

Dear Mr. James:

Thank you so much for assisting me on the highway the other night. The rain drenched not only my clothes but my spirits. Then you came along. Because of you, I was able to make it to my dying husband's bedside just before he passed away. God bless you for helping me and unselfishly serving others.

Sincerely,
Mrs. Nat King Cole

The most important thing we can involve ourselves in is service. Unselfish service to our fellowmen. It supercedes weather conditions, educational background, time commitments, financial statements, political and religious preference, and especially skin color! Serve, Serve, Serve! Three of the most important words in the world!!

The Importance Of Being Needed

Which is more important, to be loved or to be needed?

A father comes home from work and his little boy wants him to play ball with him, but the father is too busy. The father says to the son, "I'd love to play, but I have work to do. But son, I do love you." The little boy responds, "Dad, I don't want you to love me. I want you to play ball with me."

The little boy knows he is loved, but does he feel needed? No, he feels like a burden to his father. People need to be needed.

I had a friend who was getting married. Because of our friendship, she asked me to play my guitar at her wedding. I was more than willing to donate my entire evening because I was needed. At the last minute, however, the previously booked band showed up too. I had no hard feelings, but instead of staying the whole evening as I had planned, I only stayed half an hour. I left after refreshments. I still cared deeply for the couple. I knew they loved me, but I was no longer needed, so I checked out.

I challenge you to make sure we let our friends know they are needed as opposed to just letting them know they are loved. Make sure they feel they belong and have a purpose in life. Even people who know they are loved by you need to feel you need them.

An Appointment With Love

The tall clock in New York's Grand Central Station said six minutes to six. A tall young army officer named Lieutenant Blandford had waited thirteen months for this day. Before going overseas thirteen months earlier he had read a book with some personal notes made by a woman in it. He had started to send letters to the woman and she had written back. Her letters had brought him through the fear and ravages of war. As he stood waiting in the station he thought he might be in love with the girl and she might be in love with him. But she had never sent him a photograph. She said it was some kind of test.

As he thought about the letters a beautiful girl walked towards him. In her pale-green suit she was like springtime come alive. But she had no rose on as they had planned. "Going my way soldier?" she smiled.

As the girl passed, Blandford noticed a woman behind her wearing a rose as they had planned. She was past 40, with gray hair tucked in her hat. Though he was disappointed, Blandford did not hesitate. He was disappointed but he knew this older woman could become a special friend. "You must be my pen-pal, Miss Maynell. May I take you to dinner?"

The older lady smiled, "I don't know what this is all about, but a pretty young lady told me if you asked me to dinner I should tell you she's waiting in the restaurant across the street." Lt. Blandford had passed his test.

Love Takes Time

There is a fable about the villagers who agreed to contribute a sack of grain for those of their neighborhood who were ill or poor? A large vat was placed in the village square where the sacks were to be emptied. The day appointed for the opening arrived . . . the villagers assembled . . . the vat cover was lifted. It was empty. Each villager, thinking "my grain will not be missed," had failed to respond.

As in the fable, each one of us is of vital importance to the success of the whole, especially when it comes to love and loving.

The world is filled with too many of us who are inclined to indicate our love with an announcement or declaration.

True love is a process. True love requires personal action. Love must be continuing to be real. Love takes time. Too often expediency, infatuation, stimulation, persuasion, or lust are mistaken for love. How hollow, how empty if our love is no deeper than the arousal of momentary feeling or the expression in words of what is no more lasting than the time it takes to speak them. A group of college students recently indicated to me their least favorite expression to come from us as the older set is, "If there is ever anything I can do to help you, please let me know." They, as do others, much prefer actions over conversation.

Wisdom In Patience

Sometimes men, feeling offended, feeling resentful, are hasty and shortsighted, and slam doors on their own happiness and highest opportunity — sometimes even everlastingly.

No man is himself in acute sorrow. No man is himself in anger. No man is himself with feelings of offense. And decisions that will wait are safer with waiting — waiting for time to take over, for the dust to clear away, for tempers to cool, for perspective to return, for the real issues to show themselves, for the real values to reappear, for judgment to emerge and mature.

We should think seriously before we slam doors, before we burn bridges, before we saw off the limb on which we find ourselves sitting. Decisions in acute sorrow, decisions in anger, decisions under pressure, decisions that haven't been thought through are less likely to be mature and safe decisions.

Instead, exercise love and compassionate patience and allow friends to be human. Forgive and forget and learn to grow from others mistakes so you don't make them! Learn to count to ten before you act; or to one hundred and ten if needs be so as to calm down and clearly act responsibly. We're only human. We're born to make mistakes!

People Want Sympathy

Do you want to be popular and have lots of friends? Do you want to be the one who understands people?

When we are young we tend to spend a lot of time telling the world how nobody understands us. Our parents don't, our teachers don't, the people we go out with don't.

The next time you want to scream those words to someone — "YOU DON'T UNDERSTAND ME" — don't do it. Instead, ask yourself if you understand them. Take the time and effort to try to understand them and see what makes them what they are. If you do, they will make the same effort to understand you.

Try an experiment. The next time you want to tell someone your problems in search of sympathy, listen to the other person first before you unload. Once you hear their problems, you will find they are much more receptive to listening to your problems and giving you the sympathy and understanding you seek.

That's how friendships start. That's how we assist one another to turn our unsolvable problems into opportunities. No matter what people might try to make you think, most of the people you will meet in your life are hungering for sympathy and understanding, just as you are. We all yearn for someone who will understand us. Start the cycle today by understanding those around you.

A Different Kind Of Sports Hero

It had been a good year for Wallensburg High School basketball. There was plenty to cheer about at the awards assembly. Medals were being handed out, and finally there was what many considered the best prize of all, because anybody could win it. That was the award for best school spirit. Not everybody could play, but everybody could cheer, and at Wallensburg that was a big deal.

The award went to Sherri Northrup, the cheerleader with the sparkling blue eyes, the dazzling smile, and a figure that could make even the opposition cheer, despite themselves. Sherri took the stage and said: "Thank you for this honor. I'm very grateful. But I came to every game with the gang in a nice warm car. Did you know Norma Bryson came to every game, too. Only she came alone and didn't come in a car. She walked four miles, sometimes in the snow. She sat pretty much alone, but she never missed a game, and I don't know anybody who cheered louder. I'd like to give this school spirit award to Norma Bryson."

A standing ovation greeted Norma Bryson as she was led blushing to the front. She took the award with a shy smile and disappeared back into the woodwork.

A little thing? Yes. But Norma Bryson is now a grandmother, and it changed her whole life. If you want to be a sports hero, be one like Sherri Northrup.

Three Helpful Hints

Most of our opinions are different about the controversies in religion. One of my opinions is that God has a sense of humor. If you don't believe it, look at the person sitting next to you! Regardless of whether you believe in God or not, certain religion books offer three helpful hints.

1. Love your fellow men. What could possibly go wrong with that exhortation? Chances are if you loved other people first, they would be inclined to love you back.

2. Forgive your enemies. Most people have trouble with this one. Rather than forgive those who hurt us, we try to get back at them. We carry around grudges which make us tense and unproductive. Don't try to get even. It's better to get ahead. What's done is done.

3. Do unto others as you would have them do unto you. That short phrase would solve just about every problem that exists between people in the world — if we went around treating other persons the way we ourselves would want them to treat us. There aren't very many of us who would purposely hurt ourselves.

In a world full of different beliefs, let's always remember that it's still better to love our fellow men, forgive our enemies, and treat others the way we want to be treated than to live any other way.

We Become What We Are

I'm a big believer in life mottos and visual suggestion. I hope you will put this up where it can constantly remind you of mind conditioning and the importance of being a loving friend.

IF A PERSON LIVES WITH CRITICISM
He learns to condemn.
IF A PERSON LIVES WITH HOSTILITY
He learns to fight.
IF A PERSON LIVES WITH RIDICULE
He learns to be shy.
IF A PERSON LIVES WITH JEALOUSY
He learns to feel guilty.
IF A PERSON LIVES WITH TOLERANCE
He learns to be patient.
IF A PERSON LIVES WITH ENCOURAGEMENT
He learns confidence.
IF A PERSON LIVES WITH PRAISE
He learns to appreciate.
IF A PERSON LIVES WITH FAIRNESS
He learns justice.
IF A PERSON LIVES WITH SECURITY
He learns to have faith.
IF A PERSON LIVES WITH APPROVAL
He learns to like himself.
IF A PERSON LIVES WITH ACCEPTANCE
AND FRIENDSHIP
He learns to find love in the world.

SELF-ESTEEM

I Can Sleep On A Windy Night

Farmer White set out for the fair to hire another man. As he walked about, he saw a young, awkward, gawky young boy, and he stopped him.

"Well, young fellow," said Farmer White, "what is your name?"

"John, sir."

"And what do you know?"

"If you please, sir, I know how to sleep on a windy night."

"Well, that's no great recommendation," said Farmer White. "Most of my men can do that only too well now."

So Farmer White walked around the fair and talked to this one and that, but he found no farm helper that suited him. Then he met John again, asked him the same question, and got the same strange answer. "You are certainly a curious kind of farmhand, but come along to my farm."

John worked for several weeks and all went well. And then one night the wind woke up Farmer White. It hammered against buildings, tore at the haystacks, and howled down the chimneys, and when Farmer White heard it, he sat straight up in bed. He knew that wind and he jumped out of bed and shouted for John.

"John!" the farmer called, but he didn't receive an answer. So the farmer bounded up to the attic and shook John hard. "John, my lad, get up; the wind's taking everything." But John lay like a log — he never moved.

Farmer White rushed out into the windy night, expecting to see everything tumbled about. But he found the stable doors safely fastened, the windows firmly locked. He found the stackyard intact — the stacks well roped and the ropes well pegged. Then Farmer White laughed out loud. Suddenly he realized what John had meant when he said, "I can sleep on a windy night."

Be Honest

Gerhardt, a little German shepherd boy, was very, very poor. One day as he was watching his flock, a hunter came out of the woods and asked the way to the nearest village. When the boy told him, he said if he would show him the way he would be rewarded handsomely. When Gerhardt replied that he could not leave his sheep for fear they might be lost, the hunter said, "Well, what of that? They are not your sheep, and the loss of one or two would not matter to your master. I will give you more money than you have earned in a year."

When the boy still declined, the hunter said, "Then will you trust me with your sheep while you go to the village and bring me food and drink and a guide?"

The boy shook his head saying, "The sheep do not know your voice."

Angrily the hunter retorted, "Can't you trust me?"

Gerhardt reminded him that he had tried to get him to break faith with his master and asked, "How to I know that you would keep your word to me?"

Cornered, the hunter laughed and said, "I see you are a good faithful boy. I will not forget you. Show me the road and I will try to make it out by myself."

The hunter turned out to be the grand duke, and he was so pleased with Gerhardt's honesty that he later sent for him and had him educated. Though Gerhardt became a rich and powerful man, he remained honest and true.

Be Honest

"The measure of a man's real character is what he would do if he knew he would never be found out."
— *Thomas Babington Macaulay*

These words may add up to be a most useful yardstick in behavior. Not because they provide us with a way to measure others but because they provide us with a way to measure ourselves.

Few of us are asked to make the great decisions about committing nations to war or armies to battle. But all of us are called upon daily to make a host of purely personal decisions. Shall the contents of this wallet, found in the street, be pocketed or turned over to the police? Shall this order, which was intended for a rival, be allowed to register its accidental addition to your sales quota? Shall this business deal be closed in your favor without all the facts being disclosed to the unwary buyer?

Nobody will know. Nobody, that is, except you. But you have to live with yourself. And it is always better to live with someone you respect for their honesty. Remember, "If the things you do are contrary to the things you believe in, you'll never be happy!"

The Price Of A Soul

What is the worth of a soul?

At 4:45 on a Friday afternoon in April 1949, a laughing three-year-old child was playing with her small friends in a grassy vacant lot beside her home. Suddenly, she disappeared. She had fallen into a long-abandoned well. Panicked, her mother called the police and reported it. Within minutes, firemen were pumping oxygen into the small opening of the well.

Efforts to raise the little girl by rope failed, and power equipment began digging a hole. "Are you all right?" they called into the hole.

"I am," came the reply from below, then silence.

Men and machines began to move the earth away. One man stayed at his dangerous job until he collapsed with the pain of a hernia. Men on a ship at sea monitored the progress of the rescue and took up a collection among themselves. Coalminers in Denver offered help.

Fifty-three hours after Kathy's fall — after a total expenditure of half a million dollars — a man was finally lowered into the rescue shaft. While the world waited, the answer came. Kathy Fiscus — the little girl the whole world had come to know — was dead.

Is one child worth all that trouble? You bet it is! And you are worth it, too. We all are! Never forget it.

How Much Are You Worth?

At one time in his career Fred Astaire's legs were insured for 650,000 dollars. But do you think this famous dancer would have given up either one of his legs for 650,000 dollars? Of course not.

Would you be willing to part with your eyesight for a million dollars? A hand for a million dollars? Your foot for a million dollars? We are already up to three million dollars and I'm sure you haven't considered any of the offers. Money could never replace you, not any part of you. You are worth more than all the money in the world.

Do you realize that since time began there have been over 68 billion persons live on the face of the earth and there never has been a duplication. There has never been one of them exactly like you. When you are gone from the earth, no one will ever take your place. You are unique.

Maybe that is the reason there are things you like about yourself. Things you can do that no one else can do. You like yourself because you're unique. Don't spend your life thinking you want to look like or be like someone else. Instead, concentrate on the things you know and can do, the things you like about yourself and develop them. Make you the best you can be.

You are worth more than millions! Don't ever sell yourself short.

How Do We Learn?

Anyone can learn to do anything. Do you believe it? If a Japanese child can learn to speak complicated Japanese, and a Mexican can learn to speak English, can an American child raised in Japan learn to speak Japanese? I don't mean from a language teacher, but in the way each of us learned our native language — by listening to parents speak.

The answer is yes. We are products of our environment. Anyone can learn new, and change old habits through spaced repetition. Even a parakeet or parrot learns to speak English, or Japanese through spaced repetition education. Japanese or English is a far cry from bird chirps! Think what you could learn and accomplish – think what you could change for the better in your personality and character if you just decided to change and were patient enough to work hard until you developed the new habit. It's true. We learn through repetition.

If we are tone deaf and want to learn to sing, or play a musical instrument; or if we are poor in Math or English and uncoordinated in sports, it has nothing to do with ability — only maturing that ability. With determination, patience, and spaced repetition you can improve your abilities to the level you dream about. It's true. You can if you think you can — but only if you do what you think you can't.

Two Sides To Everything

Do you take the time to realize there are two sides to every story? Do you realize there are two ways to look at every situation? We must recognize the good and the bad, but understand we will get what we look for.

Remember the story of the two buckets in the well. As the one bucket came up it said, "This is surely a cold and dreary world; no matter how many times I come up full, I always go down empty!" The other bucket laughed and replied, "With me it is different; no matter how many times I go down empty, I always come up full."

Attitude determines our altitude and dictates what we get out of life. Test yourself: When you look at a glass of water do you interpret it to be half empty or half full? Are you negative or do you exercise a positive outlook on living?

Two boys were given an attitude "check up from the neck up." One was placed in a room full of beautiful toys. After a short while he was bored and inquired, "Is this it? I wanted a bike, and I'll never get that." He is a negative pessimist. The other boy was placed in a room with a pile of fresh horse maneur stacked in the middle. Before they even closed the door, the boy excitedly started picking, pulling, stomping and sifting through the maneur with a smile on his face. They inquired why? The boy answered, "When you find this much maneur there has to be a pony somewhere close by!" He is a positive optimist!

Are you negative or positive? Take charge of your life and decide to be happy!

Make Your Own Movie

Do you know anybody who doesn't go to movies? I don't. Not everybody likes every movie they see but most everybody goes. Maybe that's why producers try to reflect many different people, subjects and situations.

Every movie ever made had a writer who wrote what was going to happen and a director who made it happen the way the writer wrote it. How would you like to write and star in a movie of your own?

You already are. Every day of your life you produce your own show. You decide what happens to the main character, what he or she becomes.

You haven't finished much of your movie yet, all you've done is start it. So, think of the conclusion. Where do you want it to go? How do you want it to end? You are in control of those things. You are the director. Do you want it to be a tragedy, or a friendly and warm story? How do you see it? You can make any part better depending on the amount of effort you make as the main actor.

Do you feel good about the part of the movie that has played so far or are you unhappy with it? I know you know, and only you can decide if it suits you. If you like it, keep it up. If you're ashamed, change. Build the kind of story you really want to see. Create a role you really want to play. It's your show. Make it the best you can be.

Get Yourself Right

How complicated is the world and how impossible is it to make it a better place? Maybe not as hard as it seems.

A father came home from work one afternoon and his son wanted him to spend some time playing with him. The father knew he had work he had to get done which couldn't wait. The son was very insistent and the father had to come up with something to keep the young boy occupied.

On the coffee table lay a magazine which contained a map of the world. The father ripped the map into numerous pieces, gave the pieces to his young son and instructed him to go put the map back together.

The son left the room and the father got to work, thinking it would take a number of hours for the son to put the puzzle together. To his surprise just fifteen minutes later the son was back and the puzzle was assembled. Amazed, the father asked how he finished so quickly.

"It was easy. On the other side of the map was a picture of a man. When I got the man right, the whole world was right!"

That's how simple it is to make a better world. All you do is start with yourself and make a better you. If you get better your family gets better, they make the community better, then the city, the state and eventually the world will follow.

Try Something Different Today

Try something different today. Treat everyone you see and meet as if they were perfect. Don't be critical. Look beyond all the imperfections you are usually quick to notice.

Even if you know their personal faults and weaknesses, try and put them out of your mind. It won't be easy, but overlook the strange clothes they might be wearing today, their out-of-style haircuts or lack of height. Make yourself see them as perfect, each one a unique creation with a unique reason for being there. Don't notice all the imperfections you usually do. Realize that real beauty and character comes from within.

To make this experiment easier, do the same thing with yourself. Don't think about the things you don't like about yourself. Believe me, there are things each and every person doesn't like about himself or herself. You aren't alone. Some people think they are too fat or their ears are too big. Some have pimples. For just one day, forget all those things you don't like about yourself. Look in the mirror and really love yourself. Think about your good points and ignore what you don't like.

Psychologists tell us that after 21 to 30 days you and those you know will be better human beings. See how it makes you feel. Start today!

Birds Can Talk

Have you ever tried to teach a bird to talk? I bought a parakeet and promptly started the process. I looked the bird in the eye and said "Danny," "Danny" over and over again. Fifty repetitions a day for two straight months! Three thousand repetitions. Then it finally happened. As I was leaving the room, the parakeet blurted out "Danny."

Now it was time to teach him his last name. "Clark:" I followed the same process. It only took two hundred repetitions over a week and the bird finally said, "Clark." The learning process was speeding up!

Then something very interesting happened. I got sick and spent two days in the house coughing. The next weekend I had a party. When I showed off my talking bird, I discovered a great principle about the learning and education process. I got the bird's attention and it said "Danny" "Clark" "Cough!" Yes, the bird coughed.

Now, did I teach the bird to cough? No! It was a product of its environment and so are human beings. What goes in our minds stays and will eventually come out. How did we learn to talk, and walk, and sing, and dance?

We are not born — we are made. Therefore, if you don't like who you are and the attitudes you subscribe to, perhaps you were raised wrong? And don't be upset at the people who taught you and loved you. Just learn this lesson. If you are one way, you can definitely change and be a different way. Just change your negative environment and hang in there until you get your desired result.

Don't Wreck The World

The most popular shows on television are the SOAPS. It's because they make us feel better about ourselves. When we watch a Zack on the "Colby's" or an Abbey Ewing on "Knot's Landing" we think, "I could never do that, I'm much better than they are." In essence, what we are subconsciously doing is putting others down to elevate ourselves in our own minds. Isn't this also the reason we are negative and gossip, slander, back-bite, and bear false witness against our neighbors? We are insecure and put others down trying to make ourselves feel better and look better in the eyes of others. Ask yourself, "Are you a wrecker?"

Wreckers

I watched them tearing a building down,
A gang of men in a busy town,
With a ho-heave-ho and a lusty yell,
They swung a beam and the side wall fell.

I asked the foreman, "Are these men skilled,
And the men you'd hire if you had to build?"
He gave a laugh and said, "No, indeed!
Just common labor is all I need.
I can easily wreck in a day or two
What builders have taken a year to do."

I thought to myself, as I went my way,
Which of these roles have I tried to play?
Am I a builder who works with care,
Measuring life by the rule and square?
Am I shaping my deeds to a well-made plan,
Patiently doing the best I can?

Or am I a wrecker, who walks the town,
Content with the labor of tearing down?

— H. S. Harp

50

You Can't Please Them All

We all worry about what other people think of us. Some people worry about it so much that they never take the time to be honest with themselves. They never stop to ask themselves if they are happy with who they are and what they represent. Instead, they conduct their lives in accordance with someone else's wishes.

Don't spend your life worrying about what other people think. Sure, you want the respect of your peers, but don't try to get it through compromise. Get it through getting to know yourself and what you think. Respect from others comes as you stick to your beliefs and practice what you preach. You can't possibly be doing what you want to do with your life if you walk around worrying about the judgments other people are putting on you. You don't have to do something just because everybody else is doing it. Spend time getting to know yourself. Don't spend all your time trying to find out what everybody else expects of you. They aren't living your life for you. They aren't responsible for your successes. You are! Don't let the things other people say and do to you tie your whole life into a knot. Remember, they are just expressing their opinions, and who knows if their opinions are right?

Don't try to please everyone. Nobody has that much time in a day — or a lifetime.

Find Yourself and Be Yourself

If you are ever going to feel really good about yourself it is very important to not spend your life wanting to be someone else.

Believe me there are a lot of people who spend their whole life wanting to be someone else. In a recent poll of students 95 percent of them wished they could look like and have the talents of someone else.

Think about that for just a minute. People spend more time during their lives wishing what will never be, than they do trying to find themselves and become the best they can be. What a stupid waste of time. You aren't ever going to have anybody else's anything. You'll never have their hair, their eyes, their personality or their specific talent. A much better investment of your time is to spend it discovering who you are and what makes you special.

You'll never be happy if you just keep thinking I want to be like him or I wish I could be like her. You'll only be happy if you are working hard on becoming the best you can possibly become.

Don't spend your whole life wanting what you can't have. Spend it working on what you've got. Happiness is never found outside, but inside of you. Take time to find you and be you. You are special.

If It Comes Easy, Develop It

As you go through life, you will learn certain things come easily to you. Some people are naturally funny, some are naturally athletic, some are good in math and physics. A lot of times, just because something comes easily to us we take it for granted and think it isn't worth anything because it is so easy for us. Don't look at it that way. Rather, look at your natural gifts as opportunities. We are each given certain gifts. If we think about it, there is always something we do which comes easily to us, something we have a knack for. There is no reason to think such a gift is not worth pursuing into a career. What is no big deal to ourselves could be a real big deal to others!

I look at myself, and throughout my life it has always been easy for me to address large groups of people. A lot of people cringe at the thought of being on stage in front of thousands and talking to them. I love it and always have. Now, doing what I liked to do has become my career. It is of great importance to discover what comes naturally to you early in life and to develop that skill.

What are your special gifts? If you don't know, there are tests you can take to help discover what special tendencies you possess. Seek out a counselor and ask him or her about an aptitude test. Learn what you're good at. If you already know, develop it.

The Last Laugh

Have you ever noticed people have a laugh they use when they laugh at something that's funny and one they use when they laugh at someone just to make fun of them?

If the laughs sound different, they should, because the effect they have on people is also different. Everybody likes to be laughed at if they say something funny, but nobody likes to be laughed at for either the way they look, the clothes they wear, or the color of their skin. As a matter of fact, laughing at others for the things they can't help is one of the meanest things anyone can do to another person.

Eskimos use laughter as a punishment. If someone is caught stealing, he is laughed at by all the others in his village. As a result, there is very little stealing among Eskimos. Yes, there's no doubt about it, laughing at somebody lets them know they aren't appreciated.

If you are small enough to spend your time laughing at the misfortune of others, I feel sorry for you. You should go see the movie "Mask" about a severely deformed young man who teaches others not to laugh at him. If you are one of the ones being laughed at because of the way you look, the clothes you wear, or the ideas you have, don't feel too badly. Some of the greatest men and women in history got laughed at and worked hard enough with what they had to get the last laugh on the ones who laughed at and ridiculed them.

You Can Have "It"

Do you ever find yourself watching somebody or reading about somebody and saying to yourself, "Wow, they've really got "it." I wish I was him or her!" If so, what is "it" you think they have? What is "it" that makes a star a star in any field? Not just entertainers have "it." There are salesmen who have "it," farmers who have "it," teachers who have "it."

The "it" we are talking about is that little something extra those who have "it" put into the average task that makes them above average. That fighting heart and burning desire to be the best they can be. Following are the common denominators those who have "it" share.

They like doing what they do because what they do is matched to their natural talents. At some point in their life, they took the time to discover what they do well, pursued it, and perfected it. They decided they were going to spend more time, expend more effort and indulge in more practice upon what they realized they do best than on any other endeavor. Then they do exactly that. More than the people who are just good. They work harder on their specialty than they work at anything else.

What does all of this boil down to? Those who have "it" develop confidence. They know they are good. Not just good, but good for something.

Your Future Is Clean and Spotless

I have an announcement of great importance to anyone who has done something stupid they regret. NO MATTER WHAT YOUR PAST HAS BEEN, YOU HAVE A SPOTLESS FUTURE!

Just because you've done something wrong in the past, something you regret, doesn't mean you always have to do it or be that way. You can change! How? DON'T DO THE STUPID THING THAT YOU HATE YOURSELF FOR AGAIN IN THE FUTURE!

If you resist doing whatever it was you did in the past, you will actually begin to forget about it and feel better about yourself. That is quite an announcement. You don't have to do what makes you feel bad in the future. You can avoid it by staying away! You have the ability to make those kinds of decisions. Some people think holding on always makes one strong. Sometimes, it's letting go. Don't be afraid to avoid people, parties and situations that will not help you become the best you can be.

Too many people pay for their mistakes over and over again because they don't learn this simple little lesson. They don't gain control of their lives, and they refuse to stop doing what makes them unhappy. Stop brooding about past mistakes and start thinking about the clean slate in front of you. YOUR FUTURE IS SPOTLESSLY CLEAN, NO MATTER WHAT YOUR PAST HAS BEEN! You can make it whatever you want it to be.

The Heroes Around You

What is a hero?

A recent survey asked junior high school students who they thought were the most influential and important people of our day. To these students the overwhelming majority of their heroes were entertainers and sports heroes.

The same survey showed that society has conditioned young people to judge success on outward appearance and activities and not on inward character qualities.

Entertainers and athletes earn respect because their lives are constantly put on parade in front of us? Others become heroes doing beer commercials or underwear ads. They appear glamorous and seem to have it all, but do they really? Look closer around you to find your heroes. Surely there are people around you that you have contact with whom you admire and respect. You might admire how well they treat you or how much they seem to accomplish in their lives. Have you ever told them you admire them?

Not all heroes are celebrities. People like you, your parents, your teachers, your friends, anybody can be a hero. All it takes is to rise to the occasion and always stick to your values. It means you'll give your best shot when less would be sufficient. Yes, you too, can be a star if you're willing to do what is right. And when you do, you'll find people looking to you for inspiration, calling you their hero.

The Person and The Performance

Boston Celtics basketball star Kevin McHale was once asked by a reporter, "Have your arms always been so long?" McHale gave a funny but appropriate answer to a stupid question. "No. One day in the eleventh grade I was just sitting in class and they started to grow!"

After failing to control the opening tip-off the University of Houston basketball team ran to the wrong end of the floor in the opening seconds of a game against Louisiana State University. Stunned, the LSU Tigers picked up an easy basket, since there was no opponent at the end of the court to defend against them.

Again, a stupid thing transpired. Why accentuate these bloopers? Only to point out that there is a big difference between the person and the performance. Sure, the reporter's question to Kevin McHale was a dumb one and sure the team spaced out, but that doesn't mean the reporter was stupid or the players were meatheads. Just because a person makes a mistake or many mistakes — large or small — doesn't mean they are stupid. They are human beings — special, important, with a right to be just that — human. Part of the risk of success involves the risk of failure — the risk of saying and doing something dumb. So don't be fearful, be cheerful, and remember, the difference between the person and the performance.

Don't Wait; Get Started!

Have you ever noticed that the longer you put something off the more difficult it is to get started?

Dive in! Don't wait until things get so backed up you need a shovel to dig your way out. Jump in and attack, only then will you start to feel better. If you keep at it, the long list of things that seemed unbearable will be finished. Pick the thing you are most afraid of to start and start!

I guarantee work won't overwhelm you. Work never killed anyone. It's fear of failure and stress from delay that makes life difficult. By not starting something we only make it larger and harder each day that goes by.

An ostrich might be able to bury its head in the sand when things get tough, people can't. Some people seem to believe that by putting things off and ignoring them, a miracle will happen and they will disappear. Not so! You can't just take the remote control channel changer and press a button to make something go away.

Besides, if you think back to a time when you felt good about yourself you'll realize that the best times in your life occur when you finish something difficult and get it behind you. You always feel best when you face up to a responsibility you've been worrying about and tackle it head on.

The Importance Of Self-Esteem

Five problems cause bad behavior in young people.
1. They experience a lack of self-control. They cave into peer pressure.
2. Too many feel un-appreciated and not needed. They don't feel they belong.
3. They experience a lack of confidence and ability to cope. They want to try but are afraid of failure and don't feel capable.
4. They have a perception that they aren't making a difference. They feel their contribution is not significant or important.
5. They have a perception of "no hope." They overreact to a parent being fired or layed off. They see "no hope" in government, in the economy, and in solid relationships.

How do we combat these five problems? It boils down to self-esteem. If we take the time to realize we are special and important just the way we are; and realize we can change and grow to be better, even if our parents are divorced, or if we're poor, or adopted, or handicapped — each person is responsible for themself. Our past is gone and so should excuses be. What others say and do shouldn't affect the way we think or act. We need to take control of who we are and what we want to be. Remember, make the most of yourself — for that is all there is of you!

You Make A Difference

Have you said this lately? "What I do doesn't make a difference. I don't matter anymore." It makes me so mad when I hear people talk that way. If you're saying it we've got to do something about it, and quick.

Why does it bother me so much? Because it's crazy! Everyone matters! Every person is important! Don't say it anymore! Everytime you start talking that way you stop trying, and you will no longer take pride in your actions. I realize you want to say it when you feel like you've given your best and no one seems to care. I know sometimes you get frustrated and wonder if you have any worth as a human being. But still, don't say it. It's dangerous to even think that way!

Instead, when you get down, start saying this. I'm going to give of myself to someone and it might do more than I ever think it will. I might not be able to do everything for everyone everywhere, but I can do something for someone somewhere.

You can be the one who lifts somebody out of a dark day, makes the world seem less lonely, or adds some security to a world full of insecurity. The next time you feel you aren't contributing, just start smiling at people. When they smile back you'll know you've made a difference. Even the little things you do make you matter!

Everything Is Supposed To Be Here

Atoms and protons have never been a big deal to me. Maybe the thought of my body being composed of little particles spinning around freaks me out. I prefer to think I'm alone when I'm alone somewhere. Besides, science has always baffled me, even though I'm glad there are those who are concerned with life in its most basic elements.

I did hear, however, something relating to atoms I was able to grasp and feel good about. All matter in its simplest form is recyclable — not just aluminum cans and newspaper.

Everything that is on the earth has always been here and is necessary to making up what we know as this planet. This includes each one of us. We are supposed to be here. There is a reason for us to be here.

There may be times when some of us wonder if that is true. It is true! Each of our atoms was once something else but has now been formed into us, proving our energies have a purpose, design and reason for being on earth.

If we ever doubt this scientific fact, there are counselors and other persons who can help us know that fact is true. Remember, no matter what others might try to make you believe, your existence and purpose on earth is important. You are special. People care about what happens to you. You have a mission to perform.

Self-Esteem Resolutions

No one will ever get out of this world alive. RESOLVE therefore in the year to come to maintain a sense of values. Take care of yourself. Good health is everyone's major source of wealth. Without it, happiness is almost impossible. RESOLVE to be cheerful and helpful. People will repay you in kind. Avoid angry, abrasive persons. They are generally vengeful. Avoid zealots. They are generally humorless.

RESOLVE to listen more and to talk less. No one ever learns anything by talking. Be chary of giving advice. Wise men don't need it, and fools won't heed it.

RESOLVE to be tender with the young, compassionate with the aged, sympathetic with the striving, and tolerant of the weak and the wrong.

Sometime in life you will have been all of these. Do not equate money with success. There are many successful money-makers who are miserable failures as human beings. What counts most about success is how a man achieves it.

RESOLVE to love next year someone you didn't love this year. Love is the most enriching ingredient of life.

— Walter Scott

GOAL SETTING

Overcoming Handicaps

At age fourteen, Michael Dowling fell from the back of a wagon in a blizzard. Before his parents realized it, he had been severely frostbitten. Both of his legs had to be amputated, one at the hip, the other at the knee. His right arm and left hand were amputated as well. Not much future for a young lad like that was there? Well, in such a state he went to the board of county commissioners and told them if they would educate him he would pay them back in full.

Years later, during World War II, Mr. Dowling went to Europe to visit wounded soldiers. Standing in a hotel he spoke to a large group of bedridden soldiers that had lost an eye, a leg, an arm. He began to minimize the seriousness of their wounds and the soldiers were getting upset. In fact, they began to boo him. In response, Michael began to walk towards them telling them to set high goals for themselves and not to feel sorry for themselves. The enraged soldiers then yelled obscenities at him. Finally he sat down on a chair and took off his right leg. The soldiers calmed down a bit but they still resented him. Then he took off his left leg. The booing stopped but Michael didn't. He took off his right arm, flipped off his left hand, and there he sat, a stump of a body. Now that he had their attention. Mr. Dowling delivered a speech on taking personal responsibility for success through goal setting.

You see, Michael Dowling had become the president of one of the largest banks in Minnesota, a father of five, and U.S. Chamber of Commerce Man of the Year.

You Can If You Think You Can

The whole world watched Billy Johnson's descent down a snow-covered, icy hill in Sarajevo, Yugoslavia, in 1984 as he won the Gold Medal in the Olympic downhill.

Few people made any connection between Bill Johnson's gold medal effort of 1984 and a movie starring Robert Redford filmed in 1969 — some fifteen years earlier. In the movie called "Downhill Racer," an unknown American ski racer comes from nowhere to win a major World Cup ski race at the end of the season.

One sports reporter remembered seeing the movie years before and asked Johnson if he had seen the film. Johnson stood, the gold medal draped around his neck and the bright colors of his ski suit glistening in the sun.

Then he said: "As a kid in California I must have gone to see the movie twenty times, at least. After the first time I saw it, I said to myself I was going to live the same experience in real life. Every time I saw the movie, I saw myself doing just what the character played by Robert Redford had done in the film. I saw it and imagined it over and over in my mind. Today it happened — just like I knew it would, just like it did in the movie."

A movie put a dream in Bill Johnson's mind. By repeating the dream in his mind, he turned his dream into a reality and became an American hero. What is your dream?

As long as it is realistic (I want to lose 1500 lbs. by Friday? No way!) and as long as the dream is good, clean, pure, powerful, and positive, go for it! The only thing holding you back is the six inches between your ears. Think positive and buckle down today! Remember, You Can If You Think You Can!!

Dream To Accomplish Goals

One of my dearest friends is Larry Hall. He is a successful educator, father, and man of God. His wife, Elenore, is wonderful, and his daughter Jodi is beautiful and very talented. I love them all dearly. But the person in the family I want to tell you about is Greg – an all-American high school boy. Honorable Mention All League in football; Honorable Mention All League in basketball; starting Baseball Pitcher; 3.6+ grade point average in academics. And Greg has accomplished this as a Junior. As a Sophomore, he took a lead in the school musical. So what is the point?

In football, Greg started at Tight End. Halfway through the season, a key player was injured. Greg was unselfish and switched positions to help out the team. In basketball, Greg started until he went into a slump. He was benched. Then he got sick and missed four games. But his goal was to once again make the starting line-up. He did and helped lead his team into the playoffs. In baseball, he broke his arm mid-season and received no varsity letter. A lost dream.

Greg ran for office twice and lost twice. He had a long term goal to be named to the Oregon Basketball Congress State All-Star team and was the last postman cut. Another lost dream. He was, however, selected to the team that went to Georgetown University to compete in a national tournament. A dream come true!

I'm sure this list of awards and lost dreams will be updated several times before Greg is even out of school. So why bring all of this up? Because Greg Hall is one of the outstanding young men I know. Right now he is developing his writing and speaking skills and even has a book underway. And does he know what he is talking about? Does he rise each time he falls? Yes! He motivates and inspires all who know him. Greg has a quote on his bathroom wall that sums up his basic theory: "You gotta have a dream. If you don't have a dream, how ya gonna make a dream come true?"

I Will Do More

Have you ever had a feeling there was something positive you were going to accomplish and no one was going to stop you? That feeling is called determination and is a feeling we need to nurture and constantly possess. If you're interested in sustaining your determination, I suggest that you assimilate the following into your thought processes.

"I am only one, but I am one . . .
I cannot do everything, but I can do something.
And what I can do, that I ought to do:
And what I ought to do,
By the grace of God, I will do.
I will do more than belong — I will participate.
I will do more than care — I will help.
I will do more than believe — I will practice.
I will do more than be fair — I will be kind.
I will do more than dream — I will work.
I will do more than teach — I will inspire.
I will do more than earn — I will enrich.
I will do more than give — I will serve.
I will do more than live — I will grow.
I will do more than talk — I will act.
I will do more than be good — I will be good for something."

Every great person has discovered what they are good for, and then pursued it with determination. Try it!

Have A Dream

"Flashdance" was a film about making dreams come true. One line of dialogue was very profound. The girl has decided to give up on her dreams of dancing and miss the audition her boyfriend arranged. Her boyfriend tells her angrily: "If you give up on your dream you die!"

The reason this line stayed with me is very personal. I had a dream to play professional football, but a college football injury prevented me from being able to reach that dream. All the efforts I had made for thirteen years were shattered by a nerve injury to my shoulder. For a while I did die when I had to give up on that dream. Until I found a new dream to pursue. Going through the pain of that experience convinces me this is also true. If you don't have a dream, you die. We should all have dreams we want to strive for and obtain. Those dreams should be high, big and mighty — something greater than ourselves.

The happiest people you will meet in life are those who continued striving to obtain their dreams even after they suffered enormous setbacks — the ones who didn't quit until they got what they wanted. I challenge you to write down one of your dreams and think about what you are doing to obtain it. Then, don't just dream it, turn it into action! Make out a goal directed plan. Remember, goals are the tools we use to make our dreams come true. Goals help us tune up our talents. Don't let them rust and tarnish with time. Dream that dream today and then work to make it come true!

Is It Worth The Risk?

Robert Redford believes in taking risks. Someone asked Redford about the instant recognition and fame that go along with being a movie star. Redford replied, "I don't have any illusions of how fleeting the fame might be. We all have a few years on earth to say some things with the time we are given. The important thing is to take risks in getting those things said. If you quit taking risks, you're liable to lose everything you've worked for."

Again and again, persons at the top of their professions are forced to take risks in order to stay there. A researcher named Charles Garfield noticed that many peak performers in their sport, business, or profession have a formula they follow for taking risks. They ask themselves: "Can I survive if the risk I am about to take fails? Will I be able to go on in life if I fail?" If the answer is yes, if they feel they could survive the worst possible consequences of taking the risk, they take the risk.

To become what we want to become in life, we will all have to take certain risks which scare us. And, if we feel we can survive the consequences of taking that risk and continue on in life even if we fail. I believe we should take that unknown step that scares us so much. As long as the goal is pure, powerful, and positive and makes you stretch your inner power and outward potential, go for it. Remember, most of the time, the worst that can happen is that you fail. And what's the big deal about that?!

Think About It

There is now a sure fire way to get what you want out of life. All it requires is the ability to think and the ability to set a goal. Does a "wino" get what he wants? Sure he does! And does he know where his next bottle is coming from? No! But he always gets it!

Each one of us has the ability to get what we want and becomes what we think we can become. This is how millionaires are made, this is how bums are made, and all the people in between.

Sit there in your chair and try to figure out what it is you spend most of your time thinking about. Once you figure it out, you can count on becoming whatever it is. If you don't like what you see, start changing what you think about. It really is simple.

Any person who makes up his or her mind to reach a difficult goal has to do a lot of things to get it. But the first thing they ever do is think about it. They realize life is controlled by actions, actions are controlled by goals, goals are controlled by dreams, and dreams are controlled by our thoughts.

Getting what you want is a circle of steps that easily happen when we commit to the process of creative thinking. Start thinking about your goals and you will put yourself into action.

And remember, if you don't like what you're getting, change what you want — change what you think about!

I Wanna Be The Greatest

What is the secret ingredient to becoming a successful quarterback in the National Football League?

You have to know you want it when you're very young. Arguably, one of the best quarterbacks in the NFL is Jim McMahon of the Chicago Bears. As a leader and a passer, MaMahon guided the Bears to the Super Bowl only four years after being drafted into the NFL. It wasn't by accident Jim McMahon got there. He wanted it. He planned it. He grew up believing he was destined to become a great quarterback in the NFL. His father and he would talk about it often, and he even wrote stories about it in school.

"I still have stories Jim wrote in grade school," his mother recalls. "He believed then that he would be the greatest player who ever lived, and in his little boy writing he wrote about how many touchdowns he would throw."

It wasn't easy for McMahon. The school he wanted to play for the most, Notre Dame, wasn't interested in him. So McMahon went to Brigham Young University and broke over twenty NCAA records for passing. He then became first round draft choice by the Chicago Bears and has since lived his dreams. Every Sunday he goes out and continues to prove to himself the things he wrote about as a young boy. Each of us can do the same. To get where you want to go, know where you're going. Jim McMahon did.

Why Pigs Can't Sing

Mark Twain said, "Don't try and teach a pig to sing. It's a waste of your time, and it annoys the pig."

That's why you'll never see a pig sing. You'll never see a pig sing because it would be a waste of time to try and teach it to sing. It isn't worth it.

There is a big difference between trying to accomplish the impossible and trying to accomplish something that isn't worth accomplishing. A lot of things in life aren't worth accomplishing, yet a lot of people spend a lot of time and effort trying to do them anyway. Others spend a lot of time trying to change people who will never change.

What are you spending your valuable time working toward? Don't spend a lot of valuable time on the wrong things. When you are trying to accomplish something, ask people you know and trust if your goals are worthwhile. Consider their opinions and examine your direction. Don't waste too much of your life trying to get something that was never worth having in the first place.

Examine periodically what you are working toward. Be honest. Ask yourself if it is worth the time and effort you are putting in. Remember, you are exchanging a day of your life for it! If it is a good goal, reinforce the effort you are making to obtain it. If you find you're trying to teach pigs to sing, spend your valuable time on something else.

How Do You Imagine Yours?

We all have some kind of image of what our life is and what our life can become. What we are is something we deal with every day, what we can become is something we can use our imagination to create.

We've all heard of the singer named Sting who was once the head of the band The Police and who now makes albums on his own. Before he became known internationally as Sting, his name was Gordon Sumner. He grew up in a small town in Northern England near the sea. As a boy, Gordon Sumner used his imagination to develop a dream of what he wanted his life to become and describes it in his new film "Bring on the Night."

"At the end of my street there was a large shipyard where huge boats were built. The ships would be assembled piece by piece, becoming more massive after each step. Once they were assembled they were much too large to ever come back to that port again and had to be towed away to sea. From there they were off to see the world. I imagined myself being like one of those ships. I wanted to see the world and become too big to ever return to my small city."

Sting made it, today he gives concerts around the world. How do you imagine yourself in the future. Imagine how you would be the happiest and start working in that direction. Your imagination knows no limits.

She Thought She Could

Girls, you know the answer to this question. If a girl is five foot nine inches tall and weighs 158 pounds is she considered fat?

That's what all her friends told one overweight girl who wanted to be a model. But it didn't matter what they thought, she wanted to be a model. The girl's face was pretty but not cover girl beautiful. But she knew it could be beautiful with the right touches, it was the body she worried about.

Now there are a lot of ways to lose weight nowadays and everybody has tried something. Her research showed her the best way to lose weight was to diet and exercise. And that's what she started to do. Everybody knows how hard it is to lose weight, but everybody knows it can be done with the right kind of self-discipline, commitment, and effort. She knew it could be done.

The weight came off within a year. Underneath the chubby cheeks was a beautiful face. A face which would grace all the covers of the most famous fashion magazines in the world. A face that became the most sought after face of a decade. No model ever appeared more in the Sports Illustrated swimsuit issue. Her name is Cheryl Tiegs. The last time I checked, she got her body in shape. Her friends aren't laughing anymore!

A Self-Starter Gets Started

I want to talk about people we call self-starters — people who make things happen. How does one become a self-starter?

The first thing a self-motivated person does each day is try to gain at least one victory during the day. It doesn't have to change the world; it just has to make you feel something went right that day.

The next step is to write down a long-term goal. It must be a goal you want to achieve. Then, make a plan to achieve that goal, using the motivation acquired from all these daily victories. Watching the steps of this plan come together builds our confidence that we can achieve bigger things in the future.

Once you have the plan in your mind, the third step is to set deadlines for yourself to achieve it. Say to yourself: "I will be done by such and such a date." If you don't put time limits on yourself, time has a tendency to move on without us. We can't just tell ourselves we'll do it sometime. Things we're planning to do "sometime" never get done.

The fourth step to becoming a self-starter is to keep in mind what rewards you will gain when you achieve the goal you wrote down. If you are trying to get in shape, think of how much better your body will look.

Now, the most important step: Start today! Do it now!

We Each Have Twenty-Four Hours A Day

Are all men and women created equal? Our constitution says they are. People have argued for years about whether we are really created equal.

But in one sense we are truly equal. Every day of our lives, we each have 24 hours to use. No person has 25, and nobody ever wound up with 23. It is what we do with the 24 hours we have each day that determines how unequal we become.

Those of us who maximize the 24 hours we have each day gain on those around us who fritter away their time. If we waste the time we have, we fall behind others. It isn't something you have a choice on, either. Each hour we are either moving forward or going backward. There is no such thing as constancy. There is nothing constant about time. It is always moving, forcing us to use it. Time never waited for anybody.

It has been proven the best way to use your time is to plan your time. If you know how much time you are going to devote to each phase of your life each day, then life becomes more productive. How productive are you going to be today?

Remember, time is nothing more than a measurement of change. If we're not becoming better, we are falling behind. We can never remain the same. Don't waste your time; use it!

Look Back And Say I Won

Have you ever dreamed about making the winning basket in the state championship game? Have you ever dreamed of setting a world record at your sport? Have you ever dreamed of being a member on a championship team?

If you have, great. But remember, dreams become reality only when we go from the planning stage to the go stage. Too many of us talk big, dream big, but don't follow it up by acting big.

William James wrote: "If you will do the thing, you will have the power." Emerson told us, "Act as if and you become it." Don't just dream, act them out so they become reality. Decide what you have to do to make them real and do it. Start acting like champions and working toward the goal of champions. It's time to start paying the price you must pay to become a champion. Walk like a champion, talk like a champion, eat like a champion, work like a champion and be a champion. Vince Lombardi summed up the reward that awaits you.

"I firmly believe that any man's finest hour, his greatest fulfillment of all he holds dear, is that moment when he has worked his heart out in a good cause and lies exhausted on the field of battle . . . victorious."

Don't just talk big to look back to say, "I could have." Work today and look back to say, "I won."

Know Where You're Going

Why do so many young people suffer from boredom, indecision and lack of direction?

I know one girl who doesn't suffer from any of these afflictions. She always sticks up for her parents and friends. I asked her if she had any other secrets for keeping her life interesting and she showed me a schedule she makes up at the beginning of every week.

First, she alots time to obligations she has to do: school, homework, church activities and household jobs. She clips articles from the newspaper about upcoming activities she would like to attend, then writes notes on what she can do to help her friends during the week. She lists television shows she wants to see during the week.

From this list she formulates a weekly schedule for her valuable time. It makes time for everything she needs to do during the week and lets her know how much free time she will have to pursue activities she wants to do. She makes her list according to priorities and importance.

She also makes a list of dreams and goals. Short term goals and long term goals. The point is this girl isn't going to let life happen to her she wants to happen to it.

Organize your life. Like cleaning a messy closet, organization creates space. Organize your life and accomplish much more with!

Priorities a Principle of Time

Do you do what you're supposed to do when you're supposed to do it? Do you do what you need to do before you do what you want to do?

If you give some things in your life more importance than others you have priorities. Priorities help us keep life in perspective by giving us an order in which to do things. Priorities keep us on track to accomplish our goals. They control our lives and make each one of us different.

If you made a list of activities we all engage in, then gave the list to twelve different people and asked each person to put them in order of importance, you would undoubtedly have twelve different lists. The way we make up our list of priorities determine our character and reputation. They determine whether we succeed or fail.

What priorities of time do you have in your life?

I challenge you to spend some time on your own priorities. Determine twelve things you have to get done each week and list them in order of importance. Decide what must be done, what should be done, and what could be done if you have enough time. Then do them in this order.

Within seven days you'll see a difference in the level of success of your life. Keep going and your whole life will change. Priorities remind us: "proper prior planning prevents poor performance."

When You're Young
Gain Control – Don't Lose It

A lot can happen while you're young. You have before you your entire life, your future, you can be anything you want to be. What promise! It is also a time when things could happen that ruin your life and cause you to lose control of that bright and promising future.

The list of things that might ruin that bright future is long. An unwanted pregnancy, trouble with the law, trouble with drugs, an automobile accident due to carelessness or drunk driving are just a few of the things which could dim your bright future. Some decisions and mistakes you make when you're young you never stop paying for. They haunt you for the rest of your adult life. These things can ruin your plans for college, force you to be responsible before you're ready, make you do things you don't want to do but have to do. I really hope you believe me, I know what I am talking about. You all know what kinds of things can get you into trouble, you don't need me to spell them out. Don't be haunted by the words "I told you so." Avoid situations which could cause you to lose control of your life. Don't become a victim of circumstances which cause you to miss opportunity.

Now is a time you should gain control of yourself, not lose control of yourself and your life. Be strong. Say no to men, wine, women and songs that hold you back from becoming all you can be.

Make It Come True
(My Favorite Story)

In 1957, a ten-year-old boy in California set a goal. At the time, Jim Brown was the greatest running back ever to play pro football, and this tall, skinny boy wanted his autograph. In order to accomplish his goal, the young boy had to overcome some obstacles.

He grew up in the ghetto, he never got enough to eat. Malnutrition took its toll, and a disease called rickets forced him to wear steel splints to support his skinny, bowed-out legs. He had no money to buy a ticket to get into the game, so he waited patiently near the locker room until the game ended and Jim Brown left the field. He politely asked Brown for his autograph. As Brown signed, the boy explained, "Mr. Brown, I have your picture on my wall. I know you hold all the records. You're my idol."

Brown smiled and began to leave, but the young boy wasn't finished. He proclaimed, "Mr. Brown, one day I'm going to break every record you hold!" Brown was impressed and asked, "What is your name, son?"

The boy replied, "Orenthal James. My friends call me O.J."

O.J. Simpson went on to break all but three of the rushing records held by Jim Brown before injuries shortened his football career. Goal setting is the strongest force for human motivation. Set a goal and make it come true.

LEADERSHIP

The Key to Strength

How strong are you as an individual? How far will you really go just by yourself? How can you become more efficient and productive, while at the same time lighten your personal load, and not increase your individual output?

The story is told of a young boy who was valiantly but unsuccessfully trying to move a heavy rock to clear a pathway to his hideout. His father stood nearby and finally asked him why he wasn't using all his strength. The young boy assured his father that he was straining with all his might.

His dad quietly told him he was not using all his strength because he hadn't asked him (his father) to help. Successful individuals as well as successful managers and leaders use all their strength by recognizing, developing, and utilizing the physical, mental, and spiritual talents of all their friends, associates, and subordinates.

There is nothing wrong with asking for help from others as long as you are genuinely thankful and are willing to help them when they need added strength and assistance. Effective leaders learn to delegate; utilize all available resources, increase personal strength through synergy and involve everyone in the solution to the challenge. Commit today to use all your strength!

A Diamond In The Rough

"TO SIR WITH LOVE" is a fantastic movie for any student or teacher to rent and enjoy. A story about a black school teacher who teaches a rowdy group of students how to become adults. The jabs the students make at the teacher played by Sidney Poitier are quietly turned into gestures of respect. Even the loudest most obnoxious students are transformed by the teacher they call "Sir." "Sir" treats the students as if they have self worth and is rewarded by their cooperation and respect. Any teacher or leader must remember:

A diamond in the rough is a diamond sure enough,
And before it every sparkled it was made of diamond stuff.
But someone had to find it or it never would be found,
And someone had to grind it or it never would be ground.

But when it's found, and when it's ground,
And when it's burnished bright,
That diamond's everlastingly giving out its light.

O leaders of our young folk!
Don't say you've done enough.
It may be your rudest is
A diamond in the rough.

To weed out the "diamonds in the rough" is a leader's greatest challenge. "To Sir With Love" is a classic.

Nice Guys Finish First

What does it take to get to the top?

Some books and persons will tell you that you have to step on, abuse, and take advantage of others in order to get to the top. It's not true. Learning to get along with others is an important step to success. A flock of Canadian geese can teach us a lesson about cooperation.

Geese always fly in a V formation and one leg of the V is usually longer than the other. Have you ever wondered why? It's because one side of the V has more geese in it. Hey! And as they fly as a group, the geese regularly change positions at the head of the V. The lead goose in fighting the head wind, helps create a partial vacuum for the other geese on both sides of him. And when he gets tired, without skipping a beat, a new goose takes over the lead. Scientists have discovered in wind tunnel tests that the flock can fly 72% further as a team, than an individual goose can fly by himself. Man too can fly higher, further and faster by cooperating with his fellowmen.

Geese all take turns making it easier on each other and so should we. Sometimes we need to lead, sometimes we need to support and follow. If you want to go further in life remember Zig Ziglar's advice. "You can get everything in life you want if you help enough other people get what they want."

He Who Travels The Road Best

Once a king had a great highway built for the members of his kingdom. After it was completed, but before it was opened to the public, the king decided to have a contest. He invited as many as desired to participate. Their challenge was to see who could travel the highway best.

On the day of the contest the people came. Some of them had fine chariots, some had fine clothing, fine hairdos, or great food. Some young men came in their track clothes and ran along the highway. People traveled the highway all day, but each one, when he arrived at the end, complained to the king that there was a large pile of rocks and debris left on the road at one spot, and this got in their way and hindered their travel.

At the end of the day, a lone traveler crossed the finish line and wearily walked over to the king. He was tired and dirty, but he addressed the king with great respect and handed him a bag of gold. He explained, "I stopped along the way to clear away a pile of rocks and debris that was blocking the road. This bag of gold was under it all, and I want to return it to its rightful owner."

The king replied, "You are the rightful owner."

The traveler replied, "Oh no, this is not mine. I've never known such money."

"Oh yes, said the king, "You've earned this gold, for you won my contest. He who travels the road best is he who makes the road smoother for those who will follow."

Leadership Improvement Implies Action

Said the architect:

Oh, I've built a house like this before; I don't need plans to know the score. I've built every kind and style you can name. I've had years of experience; I know the game. So I'll build from memory; let the spirit guide. The house may not stand, but at least I've tried.

Said the highway builder:

I'm most optimistic; I have a fine crew, tons of equipment, materials too. We can build a road; make it straight and strong, to support any vehicle, short or long. Now where do we start and where does it go? Or is that essential for us to know?

The Leader said:

There's so much to be done this coming year; I've letters and manuals and instructions quite clear. Must I take all those hours to plan and prepare, or will things somehow work out, so long as I'm there?

Will it matter too much if I don't set goals?
Of course it will matter! I'm working with souls?
"If we fail to prepare — we prepare to fail."

Remember, leadership is an action word — not a title. It implies that you are doing something to lead and guide and inspire others into positive action. Calling yourself a leader and standing in the middle of a room no more makes you a leader than standing in the middle of a garage makes you a truck. It implies Action!

Seven Marks of Leadership

A true leader demonstrates:

1. The Mark of Faith.

No man, no woman ever rose to leadership without possessing faith: Faith in his fellow men, in his organization, in his purpose, and in his God.

2. The Mark of Love.

Faith without love is largely powerless; with love it is powerful. Love the work; love to do that which is required; love those whom we serve.

3. The Mark of Understanding.

Be the first to know the rules and regulations; read the manuals. Individuals who know direct the world. Inform youself of your program.

4. The Mark of Industry.

Without effort, without labor, without industry, without persistence in the doing, we are not going to achieve the goal.

5. The Mark of Self-effacement.

A leader must put himself in the background; be generous and thoughtful of associates. A leader must think only in terms of the cause. Not who, but what is right.

6. The Duty of Following.

A great leader must be a great follower. A man who cannot follow can never rise to leadership. A leader must be willing to be directed.

7. The Mark of Sincerity.

Insincerity defeats leadership. The leader sets a good example. He must be what he seems to be.

Teenage Buying Power

Most teenagers don't have a lot of money, but if you put them all together — all 29 milllion of them — they represent a lot of buying power. Last year teenagers spent over 65 billion dollars. About half of that went for things they don't use specifically for themselves, things like groceries and gas for the car. Almost half the nation's teenage girls do their family's weekly grocery shopping, because their mothers work.

If you break down what is left, it leaves about 30 billion dollars of their own money that gets spent. That's right around 80 dollars a month on items they choose. Mostly what they choose is fast food, soft drinks, deodorant, toothpaste, clothes, ice cream, bubble gum and movie tickets.

Video rentals are on the rise. More and more, instead of going out and socializing, teenagers will have get-togethers where they watch videos in groups.

More boys than girls are using home computers. But rock music has the greatest impact, with the average teenager listening to more than 20 hours of radio a week. About half watch MTV. The three most popular performers were Madonna, Bruce Springsteen, and Prince. This is a lot about teenagers' AVERAGE habits. I wonder what the leaders, shakers and doers of tomorrow are doing?

To Thine Own Self Be True

Everyone, at some time in his or her life, is going to read something or hear a quote from William Shakespeare, the famous English dramatist. One of the most famous quotes you will hear comes from Hamlet. "This above all: To thine own self be true, and it must follow, as the night the day, thou canst not then be false to any man."

That quote is a great introduction to a word and a quality called integrity. Integrity is the relationship between what we believe to be true and the way we act. People who take bribes or knuckle under to pressure and do something they know is wrong are people who have lost their integrity. Integrity is important. You can't put a price on it. It's like losing an arm, an eye, a leg. There is no set price for integrity, either. We set it according to what importance we put on being honest with ourselves.

There will be times during your life when other persons or circumstances you find yourself in will challenge the things you believe in most. You will have the choice to either do what you know is wrong or refuse — even though it might cause you inconvenience and embarrassment. But if you can resist and be true to what you really believe in, you will know you have integrity. When you have gained integrity you will be honest with yourself and those around you, and the world will be yours for the taking.

A Sense of Purpose

How's your morale lately? We always hear people in the army or on organized teams talk about raising their morale. Just what is the morale of a group of people? Let's say it's the mental and emotional condition of a group as they face the tasks at hand. Is there confidence at your school? Enthusiasm? Loyalty? A common purpose? A sense you are together working toward something? Do you support each other or tear each other down? No team or army goes anywhere fighting among themselves.

How about rules? Are you respecting the rules or breaking them? Every great ship in the Navy or championship athletic team has certain rules every member has to abide by in order for them to accomplish their goal. If those rules are broken the team suffers. Therefore, there has to be a punishment. It's the only way to keep order. We must be taught to be responsible for our actions. Relaxing rules only causes morale to drop. Every member of a team performs better if they know their job, and rules give us a sense of knowing exactly what our job is. The great leaders on any team or in any school make sure the people under them are following the rules. Any team is only as good as its leaders. Leaders set an example by following rules and encouraging others to do the same. If you want to be a great leader and improve morale, get everyone to follow the rules.

Leaders Help Those Around Them

In the movie "An Officer and a Gentleman," Richard Gere plays a cocky soldier who learns about leadership. In one scene, he is running the difficult obstacle course in record time and knows he can get the record and impress his superiors. Instead of setting the record, he stops to help another member of his class get through the course. He never gets the record, but he gets the respect of every man in his outfit.

I saw another example of leadership in 1968 during the Special Olympics track and field meet. One individual was named Kim Peek, a brain-damaged, severely handicapped boy racing in the fifty-yard dash.

Kim was racing against two other cerebral palsy victims. They were in wheelchairs. Kim was the lone runner. As the gun sounded, Kim moved quickly ahead of the other two. Twenty yards ahead and ten yards from the finish line, he turned to see how the others were coming. The girl had turned her wheelchair around and was stuck against the wall. The other boy was pushing his wheelchair backward with his feet. Kim stopped, went back and pushed the little girl across the finish line. The boy going backwards won the race. The girl took second. Kim lost. Or did he?

The greatest leader and champion doesn't always win the race but gains his recognition by serving others.

Leaders Know Words Rule The World

There is a long list of things in life we want to avoid. The number one fear of most Americans is also one of the best, quickest and most effective ways to improve your self-image.

Most people are scared to death to speak in public. A lot of people have no problem expressing themselves in private conversation but freeze at the thought of standing up and making a speech to a group of any kind. They feel like they always fall flat on their face or look foolish.

Here's a challenge. Try and look for an opportunity to speak to a group of people. Initially it might terrify you to imagine yourself standing up and having the spotlight. I speak all the time and at first it was difficult but like anything, with persistence your confidence grows. To overcome the fear, don't look at the whole crowd, talk to one person at a time, then another. If you're good with one you can be good with thousands.

Something happens inside of you when you realize people want to hear what you have to say. I started back in high school and I never thought anybody wanted to hear what I was thinking or feeling. It made me feel great when I finally knew they were listening. I was as fearful as anybody when I started. But, if you want to be a leader, you must learn to speak. Words rule the world.

MORALITY
RELATIONSHIPS

Treat Her Like A Lady

Every day there's an opportunity to treat a girl like a lady. For some reason, some guys have a double standard and don't realize girls have brothers and fathers.

We all want those who go out with our sisters to treat them well and not take advantage of them. When we go out with a girl, do we always treat her the way we would want our sister to be treated, or do we live by a double standard? Is there any difference between what's acceptable and expected from girls we go out with and what we expect for our sisters? No one wants some guy to take advantage of his sister or do something they shouldn't to her.

Here's a better example. One day you might decide to have a family of your own. There's a fifty-fifty chance if you have children you'll have a girl. How would you want that little girl treated when she grows up?

Here's the point. Do you treat girls you date like you would want somebody to treat your daughter one day? Do you treat them the way you would want somebody to treat your sister? Remember, they all have fathers and brothers who want the best for them, just as you would want the best for your sister or your daughter.

Guys, don't play with hearts of women. The true macho man treats her like a lady. Remember, love means always giving and never taking.

Girls, What Are You Advertising?

Today, let's talk about sex.

Last month I was giving a special speech on a unique topic at a high school in New York. 157 total students — 36 girls pregnant. I told the principal it wasn't a school, it was a maternity ward! After the program a young girl came up to me and asked me a question.

"Excuse me, Mr. Clark, but you talked about modesty and moral standards in your speech. Do you think my dress is too short?"

I drew myself back a bit, looked down and said, "It's either too short or you're in it too far." It looked like a wide belt!

The girl continued after blushing; "Guys always call me, and its fun to be popular, but whenever I go out on dates, all the guys want to do is park and get it on. That isn't what I'm like and definitely not what I want to be known for. Why do they call me?"

I looked closer at the young girl and had to explain.

"When a girl wears clothes so tight that it's hard for her to breathe, do you know what? The guys are having the same problem!" I saw the problem she was having. I think the boys at school believed her advertising campaign.

This girl's self-image had suffered because she had put out a message she didn't mean to convey. Girls, keep some intrigue in the way you attract men. Don't dress your body like an invitation. Show some self-respect and perhaps, as in baseball, keep the "strike zone" covered!

The Plea – By A Girl

Every girl wants to be liked for who she is and what she is. Unfortunately, it sometimes happens like this instead.

Why does it have to be like this?
Why do boys just have to kiss?
No matter the face, no matter the name,
Alone with a girl they're all the same.
And every time as it gets dark
His first impulse is to park.
Maybe he likes the lipstick taste,
Or maybe he has some time to waste;
But time like air, is warm and free
Whenever a boy's on a necking spree.
And when the wrestling match is done
You wonder who has really won.
A swell hair-do is all but shot;
Your lipstick's gone and smeared a lot.
In the dark he looks so queer
With lipstick smeared from ear to ear.
I'd like just once to meet a boy
Whose company I could enjoy;
A boy who would inspire respect
Simply because he didn't neck.

Answer To The Plea – By A Boy

Sometimes men and boys misread the signals women are putting out to us. Therefore, to answer the girls wondering why all men only want to neck:

The answer, girls, is simply this,
It's you who want to make us kiss.
You spend your coin for a new hair-do,
To win a date you simply stew.
You turn on us your warmest glance,
You pose and flirt and look so sweet,
Dry ice would melt beneath your feet.
With luscious lips and painted nails
You trap us unsuspecting males.
And so we fall, and like it too
Just like you planned for us to do.
But if a boy won't kiss and neck
You say, "Oh well, what the heck.
He's mama's little lambie pie —
You can't get thrills from such a guy."
So girls don't start to cuss us boys
To make us stop, turn off your poise.
The boys you go with neck with you
Simply because you want them to.

OPPORTUNITY

You Get What You Look For

The heights by great men reached and kept,
Were not attained by sudden flight;
But they, while their companions slept,
Were toiling upward in the night.

Despite its many benefits, work, like life itself, is seen differently by different people.

A youngster once climbed a building construction fence and saw three men laboring.

"What are you doing?" he asked the first.

"Can't you see? I'm cutting stone!" He went to the second man. "What are you doing?" he asked again.

"I'm making twenty dollars a day." The youth went on, unsatisfied to the third laborer. Again he asked "What are you doing?"

The workman straightened to his full stature, wiped the dust from his brow, took off his hat, and with eyes looking up toward heaven, he said; "I'm building a Church to God."

Each of these men had the same assigned task, but each a different viewpoint. As you move through life, you will see these three perspectives represented again and again. You will see that happiness comes from a fire that is lit from within not from the circumstances or events. To light that fire you must look for one of life's most precious secrets; that in every problem, burden, or pain that you must endure there is something to be gained – some way of turning burden into benefit. An adventure is only an inconvenience reconsidered.

Don't Shun Competition

Do you shun competition? You shouldn't! There is always a way to survive.

One family business was being harassed mercilessly by an insistent developer. The owner was Chinese, a Mr. Ling. His family had owned the cleaning shop for years, and now this developer wanted to develop a shopping center on the property he occupied.

Mr. Ling knew he wanted to do cleaning for a living, and he knew he didn't want to move from his spot, so he refused to bend for the developer. Therefore, to penalize Mr. Ling for his lack of cooperation, the developer decided to build right around him. To make matters worse, he decided to put two cleaning shops on both sides of Mr. Ling to drive him out of business.

The Ling family hadn't been in business for so many years without knowing how to compete and survive. To combat the dry cleaning shops on each side of him designed to take away his business, Mr. Ling made a giant sign and hung it above his front door. As a matter of fact, after he hung the sign Mr. Ling had more business than ever. What did the sign say? It said THIS WAY TO MAIN ENTRANCE.

There's always a way to compete and survive. Competition is good. We always rise to the level of our competition and become better because of it.

Competition Brings Out Our Best

I'm a big believer in self competition, but we still need to expose ourselves to competition against others. Competition against others is how we grow and know if we win or lose. It's a necessary success principle that pushes us to peak performance.

Two men were hiking in the mountains when they came face to face with a bear. The bear was startled, the men were startled, the bear got mad, and the men got the heck out of there! They turned and began running down the mountain trail. Suddenly one man stopped which caused the other man to stop.

"Why are you stopping?" asked one man.

"To put on my running shoes," the other replied.

"Why? You can't outrun the bear," he countered.

"I know," his partner answered. "All I have to do is outrun you!"

Don't shun competition. It breeds taking personal responsibility for our actions. It's healthy, therapeutic, and life personified. Sure there is always a winner and a loser, and no one likes to lose, but without losses, setbacks, and disappointment we would never grow — we would never have the chance to find out what we're made of.

Today

With every rising of the Sun
Think of your life as just begun,
The past has cancelled and buried deep
All yesterdays. There let them sleep.
Concern yourself with but today,
Grasp it, and teach it to obey.
You and today! A soul sublime
And the great heritage of time.
With God himself to find the twain
Go forth, brave heart! Attain! Attain!

This poem explains why we should take time to see the sights, smell the roses, practice the performance and play the game of life. It encourages to live one day at a time and to

Take Time For Ten Things

1. Take time to Work — it is the price of success.
2. Take time to Think — it is the source of power.
3. Take time to Play — it is the secret of youth.
4. Take time to Read — it is the foundation of knowledge.
5. Take time to Worship — it is the highway of reverence and washes the dust of earth from our eyes.
6. Take time to Help and Enjoy Friends — it is the source of happiness.
7. Take time to Love — it is the one sacrament of life.
8. Take time to Dream — it hitches the soul to the stars.
9. Take time to Laugh — it is the singing that helps with life's loads.
10. Take time to Plan — it is the secret of being able to have time to take time for the first nine things. You'll even have time to re-read the poem — the whole page — the entire book! Take Time Today!!

Idleness Breeds Fatigue

Those who succeed know that the criterion of a good life is growth. When the good life ceases to grow, it ceases to be good. Abraham Lincoln said "I do not think much of a man who does not know more today than he knew yesterday." Growing and learning are the only protection we have against becoming bored with life and tired of the passing of days.

Once a woman was watching a potter at
his work. His foot was kept with
never-slackening speed, turning his
swift wheel around, while the other
foot rested patiently on the ground.
When the lady said to him in sympathetic
tone, "How tired your moving foot must be!"
the man raised his eyes and said:
"No, ma'am, it isn't the foot that
moves that is tired; it is the foot
that stands still."

Constantly pursue opportunities and stay active in the flow of fast moving society. Through continual growth you will succeed.

The Hope Of The Future

If you could write a letter to the student at your desk in thirty years, what would you want to tell that person?

I hope you would want to tell that student the future is bright and you are looking forward to the opportunities for success. While you consider what to write, remember this.

Nothing is known, positively and completely. The world is full of all sorts of things to find out and do. Some things have to be done over and done right.

Every government that ever existed could be better.

There has never been a perfectly run business, school, bank, factory. You might be the one to do it.

The best picture has not yet been painted or the greatest poem written; the mightiest novel remains unwritten in somebody's mind. The most inspirational music has not yet been recorded by the musicians of our day. In science, only 2 percent of the knowable has been discovered. The study of space is in its infant stage. Millions of questions are unanswered and not yet asked in chemistry and physics. As for sports, the greatest world records will be broken every year by the young men and women of today.

With that in mind, I hope you feel there is something out there for you to discover, say, think and do. I also hope you would promise in the letter that the world thirty years from now will be a better place because of your efforts.

A Banner Year

1985 was a banner year!

A slow-running, 44-year-old gray haired man with no exceptional talent breaks Ty Cobb's all-time base-hit record of 4,191. Pete Rose goes down in baseball history.

Ed Pickney, weakened by the flu, plays the game of his life against Georgetown's Patrick Ewing as underdog Villanova wins the NCAA basketball championship.

Little-known Danny Sullivan, spins his race car 360 degrees going 200 miles an hour, and moments later wins the Indianapolis 500 in dramatic fashion.

An unknown, seventeen year-old German tennis player named Boris Becker, dives and scrambles to win Wimbledon.

A 305-pound defensive tackle nicknamed "Refrigerator" runs for a touchdown in the Super Bowl.

Wayne Gretsky wins his sixth National Hockey League MVP in a row.

Baseball pitchers Phil Niekro and Tom Seaver win their 300th victory even though Niekro is nearly fifty.

Grambling football coach Eddie Robinson sets a record for college victories. Gordon Wood, a Texas high school football coach, wins more games than any other coach.

What is the point? These are ordinary individuals with extraordinary desire, dedication and hustle. What's holding you back? When will you have your banner year?

No Free Lunches Anymore

How many people do you know who are waiting for their ship to come in and they never sent one out? Let me explain. Everyone who ever lived on earth spent time in his or her mother's womb. It was probably a pretty nice nine months — if you didn't mind the close living quarters and the poor lighting. The meals were free, you got to sleep a lot, and best of all, you had the old umbilical cord to make sure you got plenty of what you needed when you needed it.

It gives me a lot of satisfaction some nights when things get tough to pull up the old shirt, stare down at my belly button, and see that old reminder of when times were good and easy. I've gained a little weight since then so mine is getting pretty embedded.

What worries me more than the ever increasing depth of my belly button is that some people haven't realized you can't go back to that comfortable womb you came from. You can no longer get something for nothing.

We should never be tempted to crawl back in the womb, but rather realize that the cord was cut for our own good. Why is it then, so many spend their whole lives trying to plug the thing back in? The quicker and earlier everybody accepts the fact "there ain't no free lunch," the faster we can start preparing ourselves to fend for ourselves and get what we want out of life!

Self-Motivation:
The One That Really Works

Let's examine three ways people get motivated.

Fear has been used as motivation. For instance, you are threatened with punishment if you don't complete the assigned task. The do-it-or-else method.

Reward is often used to motivate people — the promise of some kind of prize to be given at the end of the completed task.

One motivation works better than the others: self-motivation — when we do something because we want to do it.

Fear motivation works temporarily. If a coach tells you to run laps, or a teacher tells you to study or else, chances are you'll do it. But if the coach and the teacher aren't around, you won't do it.

Reward motivation doesn't always work, either. Sometimes the reward simply isn't great enough to get us to work. The prize doesn't truly interest us.

Self-motivation is the only motivation that really works. It forces us to answer why we should do something, figure out what's in it for us if we do do it, and finally it helps us see how doing it will satisfy our need to feel wanted and important. Learn the joy of self-motivation — the joy of accomplishing an important goal because you wanted to do it.

Your Hometown

Bruce Springsteen is one of the hottest singers of our time. Even Ronald Reagan has applauded the work of this thirty-five-year-old superstar. His incredible album, "Born in the USA," has seen six of the songs recorded on it in the top ten hits at different times.

As I travel back and forth across the United States talking to young people, I feel like singing loudly "Born in the USA." Like Bruce Springsteen, I am proud to be living in America.

One of the last cuts on the album is an ode Springsteen sings to his old hometown where he grew up and went to school. He recognizes the importance of his roots and beginnings with pride, as we all should. At times he will even return to his hometown to give free concerts to the people who live there.

Think about what you like about your hometown and what you like about yourself. Think about those words, "Born in the USA," and how good you have it here in America. Even if you seem poor or underprivileged, realize that a newspaper boy working part-time makes more money than fifty percent of the people in the entire world. America truly is the greatest! Not everyone can sing those words, "Born in the USA," like Bruce Springsteen, but everyone can say them to themselves and be proud.

The Key

You never know who might hold the key to your future.

Years ago an old man sat playing sad and melancholy songs on a cathedral organ. He was about to be replaced as organist by a younger man. The younger man entered the cathedral. The old man reluctantly removed the key from the organ and walked to the young man to hand him the key.

The young man took the key and walked quickly to the organ. The old man had played well but the young man played with sheer genius. Music such as the world had never heard came from the organ. It filled the cathedral, the town and the countryside. This was the world's first exposure to the music of Johann Sebastian Bach. The old man listened and reflected with tears streaming down his face. "Suppose, just suppose I had not given the master the key."

The old man gave the young man the key he needed in order to become one of the world's great musicians and the young man made full use of it. He needed the key in order to share his music with the world.

Today in school, or at work, perhaps a teacher or employer will teach you something you might use as a key to your future. The greatest and most famous people in the history of the world all needed someone to teach them their skill. Somebody gave them the key to their future and they used it.

The Secret of Getting Rich

Mark Twain said "I am opposed to millionaires but it would be a dangerous position to offer me."

There's nothing wrong with being wealthy. Growth and financial increase are a part of man's unalienable rights. We should all desire more than we have and we should be able to get more than we had.

Some sad, uninformed people believe you can only get ahead at somebody else's expense. They are afraid to share anything for fear there isn't enough to go around.

The people who really get rich enrich others as well as themselves. One of the best formulas for getting rich is to remember to give every person more than you take from them. If you give more than you receive you build credit for yourself with those around you. Someday you will be able to use that credit. This is the real Law of Increase.

The people who are really successful in business, the arts or professions take out less than they are putting in.

When you start making an effort to live this way things begin to happen. People appear in your life with opportunities at the right time and the right place. People will seek you out because they know you won't take advantage of them.

If you want to get ahead, give more than you take and reap the credit you gain in the eyes of those around you.

Opportunity Exists in America

Opportunity exists in America when we bring ourselves to have the courage and self-discipline we need to succeed.

I made that realization one Saturday afternoon in New York while sharing a taxicab with another man. The man was from Leningrad, Russia. He had defected to the United States and was in the process of getting on his feet. I asked him how he liked America, and he responded: "I don't know. It's easier to live in Russia because they tell you what to do and we all make the same amount of money for doing the same job." What he was saying was he had security but no opportunity. Is this what we want?

Here in America there have always been rewards for those who worked hardest. No wonder people who live in Russia want to get out. There is no reward for extra effort – no incentive to become better today than yesterday. No reason to work harder or be smarter!

But in America, miracle success stories happen every day! People with ambition can make a comfortable living and even become wealthy and get recognized. I'm glad to live in a country where I can make a miracle out of my life, not just a living. Opportunity exists in America for those who are willing to take personal responsibility for their successes. Opportunity exists for those disciplined enough to see it and seize it.

The Modern Little Red Hen

(A two page explanation of opportunity, incentive motivation, and how America's free enterprise system works; and why it sometimes fails as socialism and communism fail.)

Once upon a time, there was a little red hen who scratched about the barnyard until she uncovered some grains of wheat. She called her neighbors and said, "If we plant this wheat, we shall have bread to eat. Who will help me plant it?"

"Not I," said the cow.

"Not I," said the duck.

"Not I," said the pig.

"Not I," said the goose.

"Then I will," said the little red hen. And she did. The wheat grew tall and ripened into golden grain. "Who will help me reap my wheat?" asked the little red hen.

"Not I," said the duck.

"Out of my classification," said the pig.

"I'd lose my seniority," said the cow.

"I'd lose my unemployment compensation," said the goose.

"Then I will," said the little red hen, and she did.

At last it came time to bake the bread. "Who will help me bake the bread?" asked the little red hen.

"That would be overtime for me," said the cow.

"I'd lose my welfare benefits," said the duck.

"I'm a dropout and never learned how," said the pig.

"If I'm to be the only helper, that's discrimination," said the goose.

"Then I will," said the little red hen.

She baked five loaves and held them up for her neighbors to see.

(more)

They all wanted some and, in fact, demanded a share. But the little red hen said, "No, I can eat the five loaves myself."

"Excess profits!" cried the cow.

"Capitalist leech!" screamed the duck.

"I demand equal rights!" yelled the goose.

And the pig just grunted. And they painted "unfair" picket signs and marched round and round the little red hen, shouting obscenities.

When the government agent came, he said to the little red hen, "You must not be greedy."

"But I earned the bread," said the little red hen.

"Exactly," said the agent. "That is the wonderful free enterprise system. Anyone in the barnyard can earn as much as he wants. But under our modern government regulations, the productive workers must divide their product with the idle."

And they lived happily ever after, including the little red hen, who smiled and clucked, "I am grateful. I am grateful."

But her neighbors wondered why she never again baked any more bread.

Where Did The Money Go?
(A two page eye-opener on inefficient government.)

Which government programs are responsible for today's debt crisis? Although it is often blamed for the massive increase in deficits and the national debt, defense spending increased only about 28% between 1964 and 1983, after being adjusted for inflation. Social program expenditures or payments to individuals, on the other hand, increased by a whopping 181%.

And that's not the worst of it. In 1965, the government discovered that there were 25 million people classified as "poor" in this country. Lyndon Johnson's "Great Society" programs were created to remedy this situation. Between 1965 and 1975, the government spent more than $1.46 trillion on an all-out war on poverty.

Then in 1975, the bureaucrats decided to measure their success. To their surprise, they still counted 25 million poor people in the U.S.A.

Undaunted, they tried again, In the nine years from 1975 through 1983, they spent another $4.01 trillion. And guess what? The number of poor people actually increased! We had not 25 million, but more than 35 million people living below the poverty level in the U.S.!

In all, the war on poverty cost taxpayers more than $5.5 trillion. And so far, poverty is winning the war.

Most of the money collected and spent to help poor people was spent on administrative expenses. Poor people never saw it!

If we had simply sent checks to each poor family of four in the country beginning in 1965, each family would have received $691,884 by 1983 — an amount equal to an annual income of $36,416 (tax free!) per year. In other words, we would have completely wiped out poverty!

114

Not only that, but that $36,000+ of tax-free money is equal to a gross income of about $47,000! In fact, if we had just sent them a check, each poor family of four would have received more net income than was shown on 78% of all tax returns filed in 1983!

These facts make David Stockman's words ring all the more true: *"What made Big Government big . . . was social insurance and the poverty programs."*

It's time to face the facts: America's social welfare programs have been a total disaster. Even worse, they must bear the major responsibility for today's debt crisis. Think about this as you decide which candidate you will vote for. Do they try to buy votes by giving away the governments money? Let's take care of the poor – not bigger government agencies and dishonest, ineffective politicians and inefficient government employees.

The Promise of America

What promise is it that draws thousands upon thousands of individuals to leave their own countries and come to America each year?

The promise exists in America that whatever has not been done yet is only what one has not yet attempted to do.

Never has the climate been better for doing the undone. We are a lucky people and have more going for us than all other countries combined. We have the highest standard of living and more successful people per capita than any nation on earth. In fact, the poor in America would be the wealthy ruling class in most countries in the world.

Don't get me wrong, success and happiness aren't measured in money, but it sure is a nice reward for hard work. In the last ten years the number of millionaires in America has tripled. Only in America does the belief still hold true that one can start out poor and become wealthy through hard work and sacrifice.

Would you want to work long and hard if your efforts weren't rewarded? Would you want to live in a place where you couldn't choose what you wanted to do with your life?

Of course not! Take the challenge to find out why America's free enterprise system is the best. Then do something in your life to preserve it.

Are You Lucky?

Are you lucky? Do good things seem to happen to you, or does it seem fortune and chance are stacked against you?

Most people live their lives as if there is a giant roulette wheel in the universe that spins out success and happiness to some and failure and misery to others. That is how they live their whole lives. They wait for a break, while all they ever say is, "Man, I just can't get a break."

On the other hand, some people seem charmed. I know a man like that. He seems to always be in the right place at the right time. I kidded him about his wealth and good fortune. "You know, you really are a lucky man." He just smiled like he knew something I didn't.

"Yes, that's true," he said. "I am a lucky man, and I'd be the first to acknowledge that fact. But you know, it's a funny thing. It seems the harder I work, the luckier I get."

People who wait for things to happen seem to get a lot of bad luck and stay mediocre. Those who are willing to work when they see opportunity always wind up being the really lucky ones. People like Charles Goodyear and Isaac Newton had been working hard on their experiments long before the lucky accidents occurred.

Hard work and luck are related, that's not a lucky coincidence. Luck is where opportunity comes face to face with preparation.

Everybody's Favorite Subject

Do you ever think about making a million dollars? Not just for yourself, but to give away to others.

Let's talk about millionaires. 410,000 persons in the United States or about 17 out of every 10,000 persons are millionaires. Some of them are young, under thirty years old. When asked to give their thoughts on "How to Strike it Rich," they said this about what it really takes.

1. Luck: If you want something, you must work hard. Don't rely on luck to pull you through. Hope for it and then work!

2. Flexibility: There are hundreds of ideas. Ideas create income. Try one, if it doesn't work, try another.

3. Dedication: It's important to work at your idea and carry it through. An idea only goes as far as you push it.

4. Money: If the idea is great and you have invested some of your own capital, somebody will give you additional money to try it. The challenge is searching to find it.

5. Employees: Treat those who work for you as important people and they will be driven to perfection like yourself.

How did these young millionaires make their money? One started selling cookies she baked. One started a high-class carpeted laundry near a university. One started selling T-shirts. One created cabbage-patch dolls. One made hats with rock stars on them. One made natural soft drinks and one started a night club in New York City.

They all agree it isn't how much money you have or how smart you are, it's how persistent you are.

Give It A Try

Some things in life probably are impossible.

The other day a group of people standing on the bank of a wide river heard a man's screaming voice.

"Lookout! Watch it!"

Turning, they were shocked to see a man in a business suit racing towards the river. They moved aside quickly as he hit the edge of the river and sprang out as far as he could, landing with a loud splash. Worried, the group moved to the bank to see if the man needed help. His head bobbed up and he swam to shore with his clothes wringing wet. One of the onlookers asked. "What on earth were you doing?"

"Well a friend of mine bet me a million dollars to one I couldn't jump the river and I just couldn't resist the impulse to at least try."

That's a crazy story, but there have always been people who look at impossibility and say to themselves. "I don't believe it, let's give it a try." Christopher Columbus sailed west one day thinking the edge of the world awaited him. Orville and Wilber Wright decided man could fly and in 1903 went 120 feet through the air.

Do you have some secret, pent-up desire inside of you to try the impossible? Don't be afraid of criticism. As long as it is good, clean, pure, powerful and positive, go for it! What was impossible yesterday could be accomplished today. You'll never know unless you try.

It Can Be Done

"Try" is not a word. You either do something or you don't. When you wake up in the morning do you "try" to put on your pants or do you put them on? Obviously you either do it or you don't. If you don't, you do it again and again to the best of your ability until you do it right and succeed.

Life has no grey areas when it comes to success and failure, winning and losing, getting ahead and falling behind. We need to eliminate "try" from our vocabulary and just do what needs to be done, when it needs to be done. And if we fail and don't do it, we need to learn why and simply do it again. It's not a matter of can't but rather a matter of won't. And if you don't, do it until you do, because you can!

"It Can't Be Done"

The man who misses all the fun
is he who says, "It can't be done."

With solemn pride he stands aloof
and greets each venture with reproof.

We'd have no radios or family cars
and no streets lit by electric stars.

We'd linger in an age of stone
without TV or telephone.

The world would sleep if things were run,
By men who say, "It can't be done."

Remember, opportunity knocks not only once, but as often as you are prepared to recognize it and are able to open the door! Do! Do It! Do It Now!

Liberty

"Let reverence of the law be breathed by every mother to the lisping babe. Let it be taught in schools, seminaries, and colleges; let it be written in primers, spelling books, and almanacs; let it be preached from pulpits, and proclaimed in legislative halls, and enforced in courts of justice; let it become the political religion of the nation."

— Abraham Lincoln

Only by obedience to law is a person truly free to advance to the height of one's ability. The laws of the Lord encompass pure truth; to learn and obey His laws (the truth) makes one truly free for the highest type of advancement. Only by self discipline and obedience to the true laws of God can one become a candidate for the greatest advancement that could be given any person.

"Only the disciplined are free."

— J. C. Penny

The world has never had a good definition of the word "Liberty." And the American people just now are much in want of one. We all declare for liberty; but in using the same word we do not mean the same thing. With some, the word liberty may mean for each man to do as he pleases with himself and the product of his labor; while with others the same word may mean for some men to do as they please with other men and the product of other men's labor. Here are two, not only different but imcompatible things, called by the same name, liberty. And it follows that each of the things is by the respective parties called by two different and imcompatible names, liberty and tyranny.

The shepherd drives the wolf from the sheep's throat, for which the sheep thanks the shepherd as his liberator, while the wolf denounces him for the same act . . . Plainly the sheep and the wolf are not agreed upon a definition of liberty. — President Abraham Lincoln

121

TAKING RESPONSIBILITY

The Control of Champions

Great champions have self-discipline. What is it?

It means you are able to control yourself in order to improve yourself. Arabian horses show it young, as colts.

These magnificent horses with intelligent eyes, well-formed heads, and flowing manes win many championships. All are beautiful specimens, but some stand above the rest. To determine which these are, they are taught to drink only when they hear a whistle. After learning, they are placed in a corral under the hottest of suns until they are more thirsty than they have ever been in their lives. Then, water is brought and placed outside the corral out of their reach, forcing them to wait even longer. Finally a gate is opened and most of the thirsty colts bolt for the trough to drink with reckless abandon. Only a few stand proud and don't give in to the terrible craving they are feeling. Only when they hear the whistle do they allow themselves to drink.

The ones who obey and resist the urge to drink are reserved for special training as champions. The other horses are lead away to live normal lives. So it is with us. The mark of a champion is not on the outside but somewhere deep in our souls where self-control resides. To gain control of yourself and become self-disciplined is the first step to becoming a champion. First, see yourself as a champion, then discipline yourself to become one.

The Desk That Moved

Have you ever been the victim of the desk that moved, or the glass door you thought was open which was really closed?

I once saw a little girl dash through her home and cut her head on the right corner of a kitchen cabinet. "Dumb, stupid cabinet," she screamed as she kicked it in anger. Now, as far as I could tell, it was the girl who ran into the cabinet. The cabinet hadn't moved.

Getting mad at an immovable object — flying into a rage when you hit your finger with a hammer or when you hit your shin with a tennis racket — is all a form of rage. We all want to scream at someone or something else when we do something to ourselves that makes us mad or causes us pain. We all have a problem blaming ourselves for the things we do wrong in life. Nevertheless, the truth is we cause most of the things, events and accidents in our lives which make us mad. Other people can't make us mad. Only we can. You are responsible for letting yourself get angry or flying into a rage.

Don't waste too much anger and rage on pain you cause yourself. Be careful before you do something that hurts you. Anyone who goes around slugging kitchen cabinets is only going to hurt his hand. And oh yeah, watch where you're going. It's definitely your fault if you get there.

Watch Out

If you have accomplished something great in sports, academics or another type of competition, I'm happy for you. But watch out!

Once we are successful, we can't slow down and glide on our past laurels. In order to first gain success and then to maintain it, we must constantly strive for excellence.

We have all seen the underdog psychology that exists in sports. When the members of a championship team begin to think of themselves as "the competition," they lose their competitive edge. They no longer have something to fight for but instead see themselves as defending a ranking or position. They feel they have arrived and have nowhere else to climb. The underdog team upsets the champion team because the underdog team is still fighting for something.

We have all seen the Rocky movies. Rocky gains the championship as an underdog. In Rocky III he loses his "eye of the tiger," the hunger he knew early in life as a struggling boxer. In order to defeat the Mr. T or Clubber Lane character, he had to return to the ghetto he came from to get his edge and toughness back, his hunger to win.

If you're already a champion, remember, every time you compete you aren't defending your championship, you're fighting for it; it's on the line. So work hard or what you worked so hard to obtain will be gone tomorrow.

Making Things Happen

Can you believe the assorted shapes and sizes people come in? God must have a great sense of humor! Just look around at the different hair colors, eye colors and noses.

People come in a lot of different shapes and sizes, but there are only three different kinds of people. First, there are people who make things happen. Second, there are those who watch things happen. And third, there are those who ask what happened? Those who make things happen direct their own lives and the course of the world. Those who watch things happen read about those who make things happen and see them on television. Those who wonder what happened let their lives be subject to whatever future those who make things happen decide they should have.

We all have the opportunity to make the choice about which category we want to be in. And yes, it is a choice. If you don't make the choice, someone will come along and make it for you. You are in the driver's seat, so take charge of your life! At first, it might seem like an awesome burden to take upon yourself the responsibility of your own life, but the sooner you do it, the more you'll be able to accomplish.

Take personal responsibility for your actions. Be disciplined enough to be a meaningful specific instead of a wandering generality. Make things happen.

Responsibility In All Areas of Life

We must learn to accept and take responsibility for our own actions. We cannot merely believe — we must do. The rules of life require that we act! Faith without works is dead!

A large neighborhood was flooded and all the homes were destroyed. A rescue boat came by to pick up a man stranded on his roof. The man explained to the rescuers, "I'm a religious man and God wil save me. No thanks. I don't need a ride."

An hour later another boat came by to rescue the man. The water was up to his waist. The man replied, "I'm a religious man and God will save me. No thanks, I don't need a ride."

Finally a helicopter came by to rescue the man. The water was up to his chin. But again the man replied, "I'm a religious man. I've done everything God required. God will save me. Go on your way."

The man soon drowned and died and quickly made an appointment to talk to God. And boy, oh boy, was he ticked off! When he finally got in to see God, he asked, "How could you let this happen to me? I kept your commandments! Why didn't you save me?"

God answered, "I sent two row boats and a helicopter, what more did you want?" In life, we will have many opportunities and several chances to accept offers and proposals for advancement. It's up to us to accept or reject the opportunities and go for it.

How Much Freedom Is Too Much?

What is freedom, and how much of it do we have? A lot of people feel too closely tied, too closely watched. They feel if they truly had freedom they could do what they please, without restrictions.

They say things like: If it's a free country, why do I have to do anything I don't want to do? Why do I have to practice? Why do I have to go to school? Why do I have to come home early or go to work, or account to anyone at all? If it really is a free country, why can't I go where I want and do what I want and take what I want?

If that's the way you're feeling you should know that lots of people have tried to live that way. But those who have tried it have usually found freedom like that eventually leads to loss of freedom. A society with no rules is a society living under anarchy, which means a complete absence of order, chaos.

True freedom only occurs when we take personal responsibility for ourselves and respect the rights of others. You can live with freedom to be lazy, to not work, to be dishonest, immoral. But remember there is no such thing as freedom from consequences if you do. You pay for the choices you make. There is a big difference between responsibility and freedom. Freedom only allows us the chance to be responsible for ourselves. Thomas Jefferson said, "If a nation expects to be ignorant and free, it expects what never was and never will be."

You Only Hurt Yourself

Who do you hurt the most when you steal? One of the world's greatest thieves knew the answer.

Arthur Barry gained his reputation during the roaring twenties. He was a jewel thief but also a connoisseur of the arts. Arthur wouldn't steal from just anybody, his victims had to have their names in the upper echelons of society. It became a status symbol among the rich to be robbed by this gentleman thief.

One night Barry was caught during a robbery and shot three times. In excruciating pain he made a miraculous escape. After escaping he swore he would never steal again. He didn't, but three years later a jealous woman turned him in and he served an eighteen year sentence in prison. When he got out he moved to a small town where no one knew him and never stole again.

Eventually reporters came to the small town to ask him questions. One reporter asked him. "You stole from a lot of people during your years as a thief, who did you steal the most from?"

Quickly Barry replied. "That's easy. I stole the most from Arthur Barry. I could have been anything, but by choosing to be a thief, I spent two thirds of my adult life behind prison bars. I robbed myself of time and the opportunity to be all that I could be."

A Police Car In The Mirror

I know of one way to make driving safer. My method would work for everybody.

The best deterrent to driving recklessly and irresponsibly is to see a policeman in your rear view mirror. Have you ever noticed how every time you see a police car you immediately hit the brakes to slow down and then check your speedometer. The second you see the police car you become more alert, more conscientious and there is no way you are going to make any mistakes. I know you know the feeling. We all do.

Can you imagine how well you would drive if you saw that police car in your rear view mirror all the time?

But instead, most of the time when you're driving, you have the radio on and the music playing while sitting in your comfortable padded seats. You don't have the thought in your mind that what you are really doing is driving a speeding bullet that can kill you or somebody else in a second.

Racing off red lights and "dragging" some guy next to you doesn't mean you have guts. It means you're immature; irresponsible and crazy! The next time someone dares you to race and says "What's the matter, no guts?" Just reply, "Yeah, I've got guts but I don't want to see them!"

Even the most beautiful car is a killer. Be responsible. Be careful!

ENDURANCE

Become Enthusiastic

What is the difference between excitement and enthusiasm? Excitement comes from momentary motivation. It is present tense, a first date; making the team; getting a good score on a test or being named to the honor roll.

Enthusiasm begins in present tense, and extends into the future tense. It lasts throughout the endeavor until the task is completed. The first date turns into a steady relationship; once you make the team you play every day to the best of your ability; once you make the honor roll you make it again and again.

As we contrast excitement with enthusiasm, obviously it's important to be excited, but it so quickly dies off we must become enthusiastic if we're ever to become successful.

Enthusiasm stems from self-motivation — from an understanding of why we're doing what we're doing. Enthusiasm comes because we know the end result is a definite bargain. We keep our sights on the goal.

Let us first see the benefits of the end; the time when the task we undertake is already done well, before we ever begin. In this way the excitement will be there to catapult us through the storm. Once we start working, that excitement will become enthusiasm and carry us through to the rainbow. Become enthusiastic as you strive to accomplish your goals. Enthusiastic endurance is a formula for a successful life.

Give Yourself Another Chance

Have you ever heard the old saying, "A lot of people die with their best music still in them?"

One of today's most popular rock stars almost made that saying come true for himself.

Starting out as a rock singer has never been easy. All of today's rock stars started out at either a beginning music lesson or alone in a room with a certain beat in their head they wanted to produce. You don't sell out Madison Square Garden at thirty bucks a ticket if you're unknown. Before you ever get that far, there are a lot of lonely nights spent singing other people's songs in smoky, stinky bars and working for tips from unappreciative customers. There were many such nights for this singer — too many. At one point he was so convinced no one would ever want to hear the songs he wrote he considered taking his own life — suicide.

But at his lowest point he wrote a song about those nights working in those clubs. He called it "The Piano Man," and it was a hit. Another hit, "Second Wind," urges us not to hate ourselves for our mistakes and tells us no matter how hopeless we might feel at times, we all deserve a second chance.

Billy Joel almost died with his best songs still inside of him. Now he exhorts us to give ourselves a second chance when we get down and out.

Keep On Shooting

If you keep shooting, you're bound to hit the target sooner or later.

Ty Cobb was thrown out more times trying to steal bases than any man in baseball history. Babe Ruth struck out more times than any man in baseball history. Hank Aaron who broke Babe Ruth's record, struck out more times than 99 percent of the players who made it to the major leagues. Before Walt Disney successfully started Walt Disney Entertainment he went broke seven times. Nobody considers these men failures. Nobody says they missed the target, because they kept shooting.

Caruso, the great opera singer, couldn't hit the high notes early in his career and his teacher advised him to quit. But he kept singing and became the greatest tenor in the world. Thomas Edison was called a dunce by his teacher, then failed over 10,000 times in his efforts to make a light bulb. Abraham Lincoln was well known for the times he failed but nobody considers him a failure. Henry Ford was broke at age forty before he started his car company. The leading salesman in any business misses more sales than other salesmen even attempt to make.

All these people succeeded because they kept at it. The only difference between a big shot and a little shot is the big shot kept on shooting.

Anybody Can Take
Just One Step

How do you do something great and noble with your life? Let me tell you about Mrs. Charles Philipia.

She wanted to raise money for charity and didn't have any means to do it herself. She was poor, retired, and lived on a very meager income from the investments she'd made during her working years. She heard about a walkathon coming up to raise money for handicapped children, and she approached local businesses with the proposal that they donate a certain amount of dollars for each mile she walked. A lot of people walked their ten miles, but Mrs. Philipia went the extra mile and then some.

This 63-year-old woman didn't just walk through the streets of her hometown. She walked from Miami, Florida, to New York City on her own two feet, a distance of over fifteen hundred miles. No buses, no hitched rides.

Reporters gathered in New York to interview her about her amazing accomplishment. They asked her how she did it, and Mr. Philipia had her answer ready: "It doesn't take courage to take just one step, and that's all I did. I just took one step, then another and another. Step by step is the only way to accomplish anything, no matter how great or small the task might be."

Mrs. Philipia was right! Noble things are accomplished step by step. Inch by inch, life is a cinch. Yard by yard it's hard!

Fighting Back

Why is it that some people, no matter how many times you tell them they can't do something, just keep trying? Everything points to the fact they can't do what they want to do, but they somehow manage to do it anyway.

There are a lot of football fans in Pittsburgh who are glad there are people like that in the world. You see, one of the players who helped Pittsburgh win four Super Bowl titles was never supposed to play football in the National Football League.

Over a decade ago, this country fought a war. One of the victims of the Vietnam War was a fellow named Rocky Blier. While in action one night, his platoon was ambushed in a rice field. At the end of the fighting one of the men dragged Rocky Blier out of a rice paddy more dead than alive. The muscles in his leg were filled with schrapnel.

Nobody gave Rocky Blier even a slight chance to ever play football again. Nobody, that is, except Rocky Blier. You see, some people like Rocky believe in fighting back, and he fought back all the way from that rice paddy in Vietnam into the starting line-up of the Pittsburgh Steelers during a decade in which they dominated pro football.

Since then, they've made a movie about Rocky Blier. It's naturally called "Fighting Back." In your life, you too should always fight back!

Hang In There

There are a lot of ways to describe the word persistence. "You're never beat until you quit." "Hang in there." "Gut it out." These seem to work a little better than persistence when things get tough. And if success is what you want, I promise things will get tough! Anything in life worth having or getting is worth working hard for. Nobody who ever succeeded ever did so without persistence through trial and error. It is impossible for real success to come easy.

Real success will only belong to those who try again after their failures, to those who simply refuse to let defeat keep them down for long, to those who believe success can be theirs if they just stay with something long enough.

Most men or women who have earned success will tell you that many times, just as they were about to reach the goal or point in their life they had worked for and had set their hearts on to achieve, the rug was pulled out from under them. They were knocked down and found themselves back at the starting line — not just once, maybe ten times. Their only alternative was to "gut it out."

If your dream excites you too much to quit, keep working at it until you can see it with your eyes and touch it in your hands. Persist until it's too late to quit.

Don't Repeat Your Mistakes

If you keep doing what you did, you'll keep getting what you got. That is a tricky little phrase I should probably repeat. If you keep doing what you did, you'll keep getting what you got. Think about what that means.

We should learn from our experiences what we should and shouldn't do. Only an idiot keeps doing something over and over again which brings him nothing but trouble.

An intelligent person doesn't keep repeating mistakes which bring failure. They learn early in life what gets them in trouble, and they don't repeat it.

Intelligent people learn to stop and make the necessary adjustments in thinking and behavior along the way. They learn to start repeating actions which they are commended and rewarded for.

If you do something which results in you being satisfied and rewarded, keep doing that thing. This is truly the formula for success!

Learn this lesson in life. You get what you do, and you got what you did. If you keep doing the same things and never change, you'll never progress.

Learn from your mistakes; don't repeat them. Everybody makes mistakes in life and pays for them. Only a fool pays for the same mistakes twice.

Fail Your Way To Success

Nobody ever gets anything right the first time. Nobody. Everyone who ever becomes a success is a miserable failure again and again. For me to say every great success was a great failure doesn't sound like great sense. But it's true. If you're not failing a few times, it means you're not pushing yourself hard enough. Failure is a very necessary step on the road to success.

All around you, people are trying to do things with their lives, and some are failing miserably — some so miserably you feel sorry for them. Don't feel so sorry for them. They know the only way to succeed is to fail. It's better to try something and fail than to never try and succeed! The only persons you should really feel sorry for are those who haven't tried anything for fear of failing or those who have tried but quit because they didn't succeed.

Remember, no one gets anything right the first time. They usually fail, realize what they did wrong, AND THEN THEY TRY AGAIN, this time with the realization of what they must avoid in order to succeed. Thomas Edison failed his way to success by discovering 10,000 ways the electric light would not work. Try to succeed at something. If you fail, consider it a blessing, not a state of misery. The secret of a failure is to learn by it, not to let it stop you. Don't worry about failing; worry if you don't.

Keep Swinging

When I was in my senior year of high school there was a boxing event we held to raise money for charity. One of my friends entered the event and got put into the ring against a bigger, much better fighter. The gymnasium was packed and after the first round Tony was getting his head knocked off by his opponent. He staggered over to the corner at the end of the round with his face swollen and asked his trainer, "Am I doing any damage?"

He tried to be as positive as he could amidst all the excitement and screaming and said, "No, but keep swinging, maybe the draft will give him a cold."

Keep swinging. That's not a bad philosophy to follow. The whole world fell in love with a boxer named Rocky who refused to quit swinging and gained the admiration of millions.

In a lot of phases of life you have to keep swinging. A few seconds, a few minutes, an extra hour of preparation when it didn't seem possible might make the difference between making it and not making it. A lot of people watch their greatest dreams disappear just because they gave up too soon. Anything worth doing in life demands constant effort, hard work and determination. You have to keep swinging no matter what happens to you, never give up! Something good will come of it.

Trials

One day a friend who was not a believer in God, stopped at the little gorge to talk to his blacksmith friend who was recently converted. Sympathizing with him in some of his current trials, the friend said, "It seems strange to me that so much affliction should come to you, just at the time when you have become a believer. I can't help wondering why it is."

The blacksmith answered, "You see the raw iron I have here to make into horse shoes. You know what I do with it? I take a piece and heat it in the fire until it is red, almost white with the heat. Then I hammer it unmercifully to shape it as I know it should be shaped. Then I plunge it into a pail of cold water to temper it. Then I heat it again and hammer it some more. And this I do until it is finished."

"But sometimes I find a piece of iron that won't stand up under this treatment. The heat and the hammering and the cold water are too much for it and it fails in the process. He pointed to a heap of scrap iron that was near the door of his shop. "When I get a piece that cannot take the shape and temper, I throw it out on the scrap heap. It will never be good for anything."

He went on, "I know that God has been holding me in the fires of affliction and I have felt life's hammer upon me. But I don't mind, if only He can bring me to what I should be. And so in all these hard times, my prayer is simply this: Try me in any way you wish, Lord, only don't throw me on the scrap heap. I'm willing to endure to the end!"

We Only Think They Are Locked

What doors in life are really closed to us and what doors do we only imagine are closed? Everybody has heard of Harry Houdini, the master magician escape artist. He often boasted he could escape from any jail in the world in less than an hour if he entered dressed in street clothes. A small town with a new jail in the British Isles took Houdini up on his challenge. When Houdini arrived, excitement was at a fever pitch and he was taken to the cell. Confidence oozed in him as the door was closed. Hidden in his belt was a tough ten inch piece of steel he used to work on the lock. At the end of thirty minutes his confident look disappeared. At the end of an hour he was drenched in perspiration. After two hours he literally collapsed against the door. The door opened. It had never been locked, except in Harry Houdini's mind. One little push would have opened it. But since he thought it was locked in his mind he believed it.

It's the same way with doors of opportunity in our life. If we think they are locked we will never be able to open them. In reality, sometimes all it takes for them to swing wide open after all our efforts seem to be failing is one extra little push. If you haven't tried pushing, try it. If you're pushing against a closed door, push harder.

Don't Give Up On A Born Loser

What can you accomplish in life if you are a born loser?

I saw the words "Born to Lose" tattoed on a young man's arm and got thinking of another born loser. He was born in total poverty. His mother died soon after he came into the world and the effects of his impoverished childhood and loneliness never left him.

He failed at almost everything he tried. His business went bankrupt, his sweetheart died, and then he made the mistake of marrying a selfish shrew who would bring him grief all his life. He wanted to be an office holder but lost election after election till finally he quit, gave it up and went home to the mediocre existence life had handed him.

But they say life is a grindstone and whether it wears you down or polishes you depends on what you're made of. Turns out he was made of high grade ore and his life of struggle and suffering failure had turned him into hardened steel. He once again returned to the political grindstone and with his unwavering courageous character, endured, won and one day his character would be just about the only thing that would hold America together.

Today, generations later, we continue to honor the name of this so-called loser, Abraham Lincoln. Never count out a so-called born loser, especially if it's yourself. Each of us was born to succeed and we will if we want to badly enough!

Ups And Downs

Did any of you grow up thinking life was a linear plane, a straight line which was always moving upward?

If you did, you're not alone. What you should know is that life is not a linear plane. It doesn't flow in a straight line – that is a false philosophy. True progression in life occurs on much more of a circular pattern. Just because things are going well doesn't necessarily mean they will always go well. If everything always ran smoothly, we would become complacent and lose the edge we had that got us ahead in the first place.

Neither is the reverse true. We can't believe if things have always gone bad they are destined to always go bad, that our problems are unsolvable. We can't just give up in that situation and say what's the use.

Look at life on more of a circular plane. A journey that has ups that make us soar, and downs that make us plummet to our lowest depths. And when you hit a devastating low, realize how you got there and don't make the same mistake again. That way the low times won't come as often and won't last as long. If you are feeling low, just hang in there a little bit longer. I guarantee good times are coming soon!

There always has to be a storm before there is a rainbow. When things get tough, don't give up! A high point might be just around the corner.

MIND POWER

The Power of Desire

Have you ever read those stories in the newspapers about normal people who, in an emergency, show incredible strength beyond what we know is humanly possible?

There are stories about women who lift cars off their children after an accident. And there's one about a normal size man who almost tore a door off a burning car to save a man's life, then related the story of how he helplessly watched his two-year-old daughter burn to death and didn't want to see it happen again to somebody else.

These stories of superhuman strength are touched off by emotions that motivate the persons to act beyond what is seemingly possible.

It's that same kind of emotion that the great successes feel. An event in their life motivates them beyond normal productivity. They don't get to the top because of who they know, but because of desire. At some point in their lives, a dream started burning in their bosom that motivated them to unleash the incredible potential we all have but don't all find. They start realizing their hidden powers and would be miserable if they settled for anything less than success. Some emotional stimulus forces them past every obstacle, no matter how many failures they have. They succeed simply because they insist on it and won't settle for anything but their superhuman best. How about you?

Positive Thinking Always Works

$2+2=4$; regardless if you think positive or negative, the answer is the same. I started weighing the possibilities. Perhaps positive thinking doesn't always make a difference. Then a man told me a story:

When I was in college, jobs were tough to find unless you graduated in the top 5% of your class. Therefore, I studied very hard. I had been up all night cramming and came running into class late. I missed the math professors' explanation. I grabbed the test, sat down at my desk, and started going at the eight problems in front of me. I finished the test with no problem and turned it in. The professor said I hadn't even attempted the two extra credit problems he had written on the chalk board. I pleaded for more time and he let me take the test home. I promised I would turn it in the following morning. I stayed up all night and finally finished one problem. I was depressed because I was out of time but turned in the unfinished test as I promised.

The next morning a knock came at my door. I answered to find my math professor. "Paul, Paul, you've made mathematics history! You missed my explanation before class that we shouldn't worry if we can't solve all the problems. Some are impossible to solve. Not even Einstein could solve them. I put two of them on the board. Paul, you solved one of the problems! How did you do it?"

Paul pondered and explained, "If I had heard your explanation that the problems were impossible, do you think I would have even tried?" "No way. I attacked them with a positive attitude and the solution finally came!"

Positive thinking does work and is an important point of every aspect of successful living. It's true. You can if you think you can!

The Power of Ideas

Ideas are more dangerous than armies.
Ideas have immortality.
Ideas cross impassable frontiers.
Ideas penetrate any Maginot Line
of conformity.

Voices can be stifled;
Men and women imprisoned;
Books burned.
But their ideas live on to torment
The executioners, jailers and censors.
— by Justice William O. Douglas

The American Federation of Teachers announced it was creating its own "Critical Thinking Project" to assist teachers to "develop and integrate critical thinking skills in the classroom."

"Critical thinking" is the ability to reason, identify assumptions, analyze arguments, understand inferences and formulate conclusions.

"An implicit ideal of the schools is to prepare students to meet the challenges of their world, to ready them for productive satisfying lives and effective participation in a democratic society. But, many high school students do not possess the higher-order intellectual skills."

Studies have found, "Forty percent of students cannot draw simple inferences, 80 percent cannot write a persuasive essay, 66 percent cannot solve a math problem requiring several steps."

The AFT survey showed that 26 states and Puerto Rico are now taking steps to initiate reforms geared to bolster critical thinking skills.

For example, the California state college and university system has instituted a graduation requirement in critical thinking for all students.

And in Pennsylvania, the AFT survey said, "Thinking is one of the state's 12 educational goals.

147

As A Man Thinketh

People always told me as I grew up, "You become what you think about." Now, that's not true. If that were true, I would have been a woman by the time I was twelve years old! We don't become what we think about, but what we think about becoming.

I never met anyone who thought about becoming nothing who didn't make it. Everyone I ever met who said they didn't want to be anything wound up being nothing. On the other hand, I know a lot of people who thought about becoming doctors, educators and lawyers and they succeeded! I've known people who wanted to become athletes who became athletes.

Who and what we become is a direct result of who and what we think we can become. Start thinking about becoming something. If you already know what you want to be, start seeing yourself visually as that person. Visualize it again and again in your mind. Your mind will start telling you how to become what you are thinking about.

If you don't like the person you are becoming, change. The way you change yourself and the circumstances around you is to change what goes into your mind. If you want to achieve success and accomplish something, make it an obsession. Start thinking about it. Knowing what you want to become means you're already half way there!

Charging Your Mind

Nearly a century ago, Professor Henry made his famous experiment with a charged magnet, which revolutionized the electrical practice of his age. First, he took an ordinary magnet of large size, suspended it from a rafter, and lifted a few hundred pounds of iron. Then he wrapped the magnet with wire and charged it with the current from a small battery. Instead of only a few hundred, the now charged magnet lifted three thousand pounds.

It is estimated that we use but one-tenth of the powers of our mind. The other nine-tenths lie dormant. For some reason the other nine-tenths just never get charged.

There are ways to charge a mind working at just one-tenth capacity. The man or woman who charges their mind with proper training and lively community interests and activities multiplies their everyday powers far above average. Like a charged magnet, a charged mind is so much more powerful than the ordinary one. But you have to want to charge your mind yourself.

Nobody will ever gain strength by weakening the strong. You can't help the poor by destroying the rich. You cannot help anybody by permanently doing for them what they could and should do for themselves. Only you can charge your mind and make it powerful. No one can do it for you. Only you can charge yourself. Challenge yourself to make your mind more powerful, for you.

Technology Can't Do Everything

Even a car with the fanciest computer programming can't do everything.

A wealthy foreign student, new to America and impressed by the technology around him, bought a new van loaded with all the modern extras.

The next day he suffered a near fatal accident and was lucky to survive. There seemed to be no apparent reason for the van to go off the freeway. There was only a slight turn in the road. By talking to the young man, the police found out what had happened. It seemed the foreign student thought the cruise control button did more than regulate the speed of the van. He thought it would allow the van to drive and steer itself. He had pushed the cruise control button while driving on the freeway and had gone in the back of the van to get a soft drink from the refrigerator. You can figure out the rest.

Even the most sophisticated electrical computer can only do what it is programmed to do. We talk a lot today about programming computers. I wish we spent more time programming our minds. Our minds are the most complex and capable computers around, despite the advancements electrical computers have made. Our minds can do anything we program them to do. What are you telling your mind to do?

Stretch Your Mind

Have you ever heard any great sports stories about the guy who reached back and gave it something extra when he thought he had nothing left?

I've got a million of those, this isn't one of them.

There are other kinds of fatigue not related to incredible athletic victories. Our minds have a second wind just like our bodies. We can learn to force ourselves to stretch the potential of our minds in the same way athletes stretch their physical potential. When we feel mental fatigue we need to force ourselves to continue in order to maximize our mental resources. We have to endure.

Next time you feel bushed mentally and feel you can't go on, force yourself to continue working. If you keep pushing I guarantee you'll break through and feel renewed. It should only take minutes. Mental fatigue is only temporary.

What is the challenge? Start today to use the ninety percent of your mind most of us never tap. The only way you'll ever discover your mental second wind is to prove it by striving for mental toughness and reaching for something extra as you seek excellence in everything you do.

Just think, one day they could be setting world record standards for mind activity according to percentage of capacity used in a lifetime. In a race like that, men and women could truly go head to head.

Practice In Your Mind

Any of you who play golf know the importance of practice. Would you believe a golfer who had never shot better than the low nineties, quit for seven years, only to shoot 74 the first time he played again. Major Nesmeth spent those seven years in a small cage four and a half feet tall in a North Vietnam prisoner of war camp. How did he do it?

For the seven years he sat in that cage he had to imagine something just to keep from going insane. He imagined himself playing golf as he sat in his cage. He imagined everything to the last detail, his golf clothes, the grass, the trees. He saw the way he held the club as he lectured himself to hold his arms correctly, his head still, and keep his eye on the ball. He saw himself swinging smooth and following through as his imaginary ball flew down the fairway. He did this on every shot, imagined a perfect shot.

For seven days a week for seven full years he played 18 holes of perfect golf and never missed a shot while he occupied valuable hours sitting in his prison cell trying to survive.

If you want to reach your goal, you must see yourself reaching it in your mind over and over before you actually arrive there. Major Nesmeth did. So can you.

We Put The Barriers There

Do you spend time thinking about reasons you can't do things, about obstacles in your way to obtaining what you need and want? Henry Ford of Ford Motor said: "One of the great discoveries a man or woman makes and one of the greatest surprises they ever enjoy is when they find out they can do what they were afraid they couldn't do. Most of the barriers we beat our heads against and worry about were put there by us, and only we can take them down."

Of all the barriers, there are three that plague everyone. First, we get distracted. We have great plans and goals, but we don't set aside time to work for them. We watch television shows we won't remember the next day. We "hang out" instead of work toward something. Small distractions add up.

The second barrier: We tell ourselves tomorrow will be better. We put off starting something thinking there will be more time tomorrow or next week. There never is.

The third barrier is the worst – we lose faith in ourselves. We begin to feel we aren't as competent as we thought we were. We listen to every criticism and dwell on our every mistake. We lower our expectations.

These barriers we cause ourselves. It is up to us to overcome them. Don't procrastinate, do! Overcome mental barriers by going ahead with what you're afraid to do.

Programming Your Mind

Your mind is a computer being constantly programmed. If you program in thoughts like "I can't. I'm lazy, I'm fat, I'm ugly," you begin to feel that way. You get out what you put in, your computer starts to believe what you are telling it. You act like a loser, say stupid things, eat too much and act immature. Even worse, you start to not like yourself. You can't help it because that is the way you programmed your mind. It's what you put in.

Put positive things into your most personal computer. Tell your mind you are pretty, smart, and that you like yourself. Your mind will begin to believe it. Remember, it can only do what you tell it to do, so program your mind the way you want it to be. Concentrate on things you like about yourself and feed them into your subconscious mind. It only takes thirty days to reprogram your entire thinking process and change negative thoughts to positive thoughts.

Write down what you want to be on a piece of paper. Read it several times each day to keep it in your thoughts. Your subconscious mind will eventually make you start to believe it and act like it. Try it. You don't have to be shy, fat, clumsy, stupid or any other negative way you don't want to be. Think positive and program yourself to be the person of your dreams. You can make it happen.

What You See Is What You Think You See

As you put the finishing touches on your hair in the mirror, consider this question: What are you?

I can already tell you the answer to that question. We all are what we think we are. We aren't what people tell us we are. The way we see ourselves determines if we ever become champions. We must first see ourselves as champions.

There are champions all around us. We hear stories about champions almost daily. There are champions in every field — sports, music, school, business and service to others. All of us have the tools to be champions. Whether we use them or not is our choice. We can reach our ultimate capacity or let our talents rust.

Champions aren't born; they are made through hard work and determination. They are made of fighting hearts and burning desires. They are made when an individual discovers his own ability and decides to do what he can do in the best way he knows how. In other words champions give it everything they've got when less would be sufficient.

Watch some of the champions in the world, and start to notice what it takes to be a champion. Your life should mean a great deal to you. Even though you and I might have come to America on different ships, we're all in the same boat now. We all want to succeed, to become champions. Start seeing yourself as a champion in that mirror.

Before Eagles Fly

Why do we take a lot of different subjects in school?

If animals had a school and they taught, say, running, climbing, flying and swimming — and all the animals had to take every subject — there might be some problems.

It's a cinch the duck would be great in swimming — probably better than his teacher — but he'd be a disaster at running, and practicing would ruin his webbed feet which made him so good at swimming in the first place.

The rabbits would get 'A's' in running, but they'd probably drown before they learned how to swim very well.

A squirrel could easily get an 'A' in climbing, but only get a 'C' or 'D' in flying.

"So why do I need algebra?" you ask yourself.

You think some people might need it, but once you can add, subtract, multiply and divide, you can handle daily life. I won't need algebra if I'm a hotel manager, or a writer, or an attorney, or in a lot of the thirty thousand different careers available. If ducks don't need to learn to run, and gophers don't need to fly, why make an eagle walk when it flies so majestically. Why?

The reason is that even eagles walked before they flew. Spend extra time in the area of your major talent, but try them all while you have the chance. Now is the time of life to discover what you do best.

APPRECIATION

Being Thankful

How many times today will you thank someone for their help or tell someone they are greatly appreciated. There are a lot of unsung heroes walking the halls of life and how many do we take for granted? If your building is fresh and clean — who's responsible? If your food is good — who's responsible? If your ride to school is pleasant and safe — who's responsible?

My point is this — it's a shame the only time we notice a clean bathroom is when we have to use a dirty one. It's a shame the only time we notice good service and food is after it is bad. Therefore, let's learn to be grateful without having a negative experience to wake us up. Let's perfect the art of graciousness and truly recognize the contributions each person makes every day. All of us are better off because we contribute our expertise to the common cause. Each of us constitutes one piece of the big puzzle. Custodians are just as important as the teachers. Teachers are just as important as food service workers. Bus drivers and car pool people are just as important as students. Students are just as important as all of the above, and the cycle continues. Each person is an integral part of the big machine. Don't let anyone go unnoticed. We can't afford to take anyone or any service for granted. Start today and be warm, friendly and thankful to everyone.

Feel Thankful

Do you feel the world owes you a living? Or, are you thankful for the things you have and the people around you?

I'm not saying you have to like everything about your life. I'm asking if there are a lot of things you just take for granted and figure you've got coming to you.

The world doesn't owe anybody anything! Be grateful for a chance to learn and earn! For good health! For people who love you!

The extent to which people are grateful in life has a lot to do with the amount of happiness they achieve. Grateful people carry with them an aura of good cheer and well-being.

I'm not even talking about optimism here. Realize that ugly terrible things go on around you all the time, but feel grateful when those terrible things don't happen to you. If terrible things do happen realize they are only temporary and won't last forever. Happy people spend more time being thankful for all the good things they have than they do being preoccupied with the unpleasant things of life. Expect the best from life and as you do you'll find yourself getting it almost ninety percent of the time. Enjoy the food you eat, the time you have to sleep, the people around you, even the work you have to do. Take time to smell the roses and love life. You'll be grateful if you do.

The Two Most Important Words

There are two very important words we all have to use if we want to have a lot of friends and be popular. How often do you use these two words? Say them to yourself and see if it sounds familiar. "Thank You."

You don't have to hold up a clenched fist in the air, or give the thumbs up to gesture your appreciation. In any case a "Thank You," will get the job done just as well.

I'm not saying when somebody does us a favor we should fall to our knees and give them praise. All I'm saying is we should thank them politely.

Some people haven't learned the value of those words and don't use them regularly. There's an easy way to remind somebody who forgets to say them. Say, "You're Welcome," and· you'll be surprised how many people you can get to say "Thank You." They might be a little startled or embarrassed when they realize you are reminding them, but most of them will get the point.

It doesn't cost anything to be nice and polite. Most people would much rather complain and criticize than show appreciation. Most people notice the things that are wrong around them and not the gestures of kindness being offered to them.

If I were you, I'd say, "Thank You" wherever and whenever I could.

159

LISTENING

Learn By Listening

One of life's most embarrassing moments has happened to all of us. The moment the teacher calls on you and you don't know what he's talking about because you were talking. You were talking when you should have been listening. Why is learning to listen so important? Because you can't learn much with your own mouth open. Whatever you have to say has to be something you already know.

A high-school teacher was asked by one of his students who was eager to learn, what the best secret to learning was.

"What is the secret to learning?"

The professor held up his finger as if to quiet the young man and then said quietly. "Listen."

A minute passed and the student grew impatient for his answer.

"Well, I'm listening."

The teacher replied "That is the secret."

That teacher was right. When you study by yourself you can learn by listening to the words on the pages. When you're in the classroom you learn by listening. If you listen to your teacher you'll learn something you don't already know. You'll never learn all you need to know in life if all you do is talk.

Are You Hard of Hearing

Are a lot of people telling you things like: "How many times do I have to tell you?" or "Are you hard of hearing?" Maybe there's a reason. Maybe their frustration with your inability to understand is merited.

Before you begin checking your ears for wax or start worrying that maybe you are playing your music too loud, let's look at another possible solution.

Maybe you aren't concentrating on what you are being told. To use another one of those sayings, maybe it "goes in one ear and out the other" without ever being imprinted on the pathways of your brain.

Let's talk about the mental art of listening. One of the most valuable arts you will ever learn in your life is the art of really hearing what it is other people are trying to tell you. You can never remember what other people are saying if you are just formulating in your mind what you are going to reply as they talk. Therefore, listen to capture and understand, not to respond. Concentrate on what other people are trying to say to you. Let it register in your mind. Listen as though you will be asked to repeat it to someone else. Nobody likes to hear something over and over again, and nobody likes to tell people the same thing over and over again. So get it right the first time. Listen — don't just hear!

The Conversation Hog

Do you know any conversation hogs? People who never let anyone else talk. They seem to have a strong opinion on just about everything. You could throw them any subject and they would babble on as if they were the authority on it, never letting anyone get in a word.

Here's a big secret about having and keeping friends. Most people like to talk about themselves and they want somebody to listen to them. If you are doing too much of the talking, you'll see the other person's attention start to wander. Don't take more of a conversation than your fair share. If you want to have friends and influence people, ask questions that get others to talk about themselves.

You don't accomplish anything by always talking about yourself but you'll be surprised how popular you become by showing an interest in what the other person is saying and doing. If you make him or her feel like they are important to you, you'll see instant friendships starting.

Don't look at every conversation you have as a chance to talk about yourself, and what you are wanting and doing. Instead, try to listen and learn. When others are talking, don't just be reloading your own mouth to talk, let them know you hear what they're saying. Listen to learn. People don't care how much you know until they know how much you care.

Know-It-Alls

Do you know any know-it-alls?

You know, the type of guy or girl who act like they know everything, who act like, "Hey, there is nothing you can teach me because I'm too cool. There is nothing new under the sun that I don't know."

They don't know everything — no one does! The people who think they do are the biggest fools of all. They are missing out on learning, on progressing.

They're easy to spot. They walk around with their hands in their pockets, maybe lean back against the wall with their head tilted back a little, use big words to talk about little things and ignore those around them. They think the image of the experienced, sophisticated, "I'm-too-good-for-this" look makes them look smarter, cooler. But they are wrong. It's all an act based on insecurity.

What they've really done is strangled their enthusiasm. They've let themselves become dull, life has become boring. If you're feeling that way, get the zest back in your life. Realize there is still a lot to see in the world and a lot to learn. Get interested in something you don't know everything about. Become green again. Green things keep growing — ripe things go rotten.

COMMUNICATE
BE POSITIVE

Say It Right

I don't think the importance of communicating with persons we're involved with can be stressed enough. I remember one time I really blew it when some well-chosen words could have really scored some points for me.

I was face to face with Felicia Gardner, the most beautiful girl in school. I was only a freshman. She was a junior, and she went out with me. At dinner in the swank restaurant, the candles were burning and she never looked better. I just had to tell her how beautiful she looked. I leaned across the table, making sure not to catch my hair or my rented tuxedo on fire as I bent closer. I wanted to say "Felicia, your face makes time stand still." It didn't quite come out that way. Instead I said, "Felicia, you've got a face that would stop a clock."

Felicia called me a wisemouth, dumb jock and left the table crying. I lost Felicia Gardner and was left with a sixty-dollar dinner bill.

It doesn't take much to ruin a relationship, even a relationship that is important. All relationships are successful or unsuccessful depending on how well we communicate. Choose your words wisely, or suffer the consequences. There is a right way and a wrong way to say the same thing — and yes, it does make a difference to those we care about.

Give Praise
It Only Comes Back To You

I'll bet you don't like to go without recognition when you've done something good. Nobody does! Everybody likes to be appreciated.

I'm sure we can all remember times when somebody went to extra pains to let us know we were appreciated. You know the type. Maybe a teacher went out of their way to say "atta boy," or "atta girl," for a job well done.

Well, the time has now come for us to do the same. It's time for us to look for opportunities every day to give people this special something they need the most. It's time to pass along a little praise!

The need for praise is basic to everyone. When they get it a person grows. Without it people tend to shrink and withdraw. Look for the occasion to give an encouraging word or compliment. Constantly strive to make people feel wanted and important. As you do, it not only helps others, but also forces us to concentrate on what is right with people and not on what's wrong with them. This keeps us positive, makes us more productive and pleasant to be around, and we attract a larger circle of friends. Another great thing about praise. If you give it, you receive it.

If plants grow from sunlight, people grow from praise. Give praise to others, its the climate we all grow best in. Remember the goal – try to catch somebody doing something right!

166

Piling On

In football there is a penalty for what is called, "piling on." "Piling on," occurs when players on the opposing team continue hitting a man when he is down. The penalty for "piling on" is fifteen yards, and is called a personal foul for "unnecessary roughness." But football players aren't the only ones who pile on or show unnecessary roughness to others.

Some people like to "pile on" with their mouths. They just keep piling criticism on somebody who is already down and out, just to push them a little deeper into misery. Are you guilty of piling on lately?

There are times some things should be said and other times to keep silent. Do you make cutting comments to people when simple kindness suggests it would be better to be silent? Perhaps they've already heard enough? If somebody makes a mistake and knows it, are you one who has to pile it on to embarrass them more than they are already embarrassed?

Have the good sense to know what to say, when to say it, and when to be silent. Cutting, mean comments do irreparable damage to people. People get hurt when they get attacked in groups, just like football players. Remember, chastise in private — praise in public.

The Way You Treat People

Let's consider what effect your attitude has on people whose lives you touch.

One lucky teacher was told he would be working with the genius kids. He was told they were so unbelievably bright they would answer questions before they were asked. He was also warned they were so bright they would try and fool him. Some of them were lazy and would try and con him into giving less work.

Don't listen to them he was told. They can work. Just put it to them. Some might even say "Teacher that's too hard." Don't listen to them he was told and don't worry about the problems being too hard. These kids can solve the toughest ones if you give them your vote of confidence, love, discipline, genuine interest, and proper instruction.

Another teacher was told "You have the average kids. They're not too bright nor too dumb. We expect average results from them."

At the end of the year the first group of students had moved a year ahead of the second group. Why? In reality, there were no genius students, they were all average. The first group was only treated like geniuses. They were given something to live up to and not something to live down to.

The way you see somebody is the way you treat them and the way you treat them is the way they often become.

The Three Hardest Words To Say

What is the most difficult three-word phrase we ever have to say to another person?

It isn't "I love you." Believe it or not, some people even have problems with that one.

I'm going to keep you guessing for a minute while I explain something you ought to know for your own good.

Surveys indicate the man on the street or the lady in the hair salon, or the kid in the hall who tells you something is wrong ninety-nine percent of the time. They are telling you something they heard from another person who didn't know what they were talking about. Rumors start that way. They aren't founded on truth in the first place. Get your information from sources you can depend on. Don't pass on stories you aren't sure are true unless you hear it from someone you know isn't wrong.

If you do that, you'll spend a lot less time saying the three words we all have the most trouble owning up to — the three words we all absolutely dread and never want to say. They are hard to say to our friends, to our parents, and even to ourselves. What are they? Simple: "I was wrong."

Those words are hard to say, but by saying them you become right. If you're wrong and you know it, admit it. If you hear something you aren't sure is true, don't spread it. Then you won't ever have to admit you're wrong.

Don't Put People Down

Why do we put other people down?

We all like to root for the underdog — the struggling person trying hard to succeed but who hasn't quite managed to get there yet. We all feel sorry for failures.

A funny thing happens to us when that failure suddenly becomes a success. We start to resent their success. Why is it so hard to share in the success of others. Instead of being happy for them, we often tear them down after they "make it." If we can understand what makes us do that, we can understand the major reasons we put people down.

When we see people succeed, it makes us feel insecure. Instead of learning from them and trying to follow their example, we become jealous, try to avoid them, and start hoping they stumble.

Don't be too small or too petty to acknowledge and share in the success of another. Don't start saying bad things or looking for faults in a successful person. Don't think by putting someone down you'll feel any better. If you want to watch someone who spreads stories about others, watch J.R. on "Dallas" or Joan Collins on "Dynasty." They are prime examples of persons who try to feel better by putting others down. Millions of persons in America watch those shows weekly just to despise these two story spreaders who try to ruin those around them.

The Breakfast Club

Every school has its different social groups. Each student has his or her own special problems. This became evident in the movie, "The Breakfast Club." It was based on the different social groups coming together. The five stars play five students who are being punished by having to spend their entire Saturday in the school library for disciplinary reasons.

One student is a true hoodlum and a drug user. One is a very studious straight-A, straight-laced member of the math club. The third male is a jock on the school wrestling team. There are two girls, one the prom queen prizzy type and the other a loner afraid to speak to those around her.

What this unlikely group comes to realize is they are all human with problems which bother them deeply. They all have problems pleasing their parents and dealing with growing up. By sharing their problems they become very close for that one day they are forced to spend together.

At the end of the day they realize as much as they like each other, come Monday at school, they won't be able to treat each other as friends. Their friends won't accept them for liking people from other groups.

When the movie ends we are hoping they can go back to school and remain friends despite their different social groups. We're all people with problems no matter who we hang out with. Don't let friends keep you from friends. We may look different on the outside, but inside we're all basically the same.

WORRY, PROBLEMS & PAIN

Joy Follows Pain

Carol Burnett was once asked to describe a labor pain. She said, "If you want to know what it feels like to have a baby, grab your bottom lip and pull it over your head." Ouch! And she wasn't kidding, either.

The joy of having a child and holding it in a woman's arms is preceded by the incredibly painful process known as labor. First pain, then joy. Oftentimes in life, the greatest joys we feel are preceded by an intense period of pain and suffering. What we want the most in life sometimes necessitates that we suffer in order to obtain it. A scholarship, whether it be scholastic or athletic, is preceded by hard, painful work, study and training. You've heard the coach yell, "No pain, no gain." Well, it's true! The joy and satisfaction we obtain after going through the pain to acquire what we want the most makes the pain worth the effort.

The famous painter, Renoir, continued to paint even though his hands were gnarled and hurting. He explained it this way: "The pain is only momentary, but the beauty will remain." If you asked Carol Burnett the same question about her child, she would probably say the same thing. There are a lot of things in life worth suffering pain to obtain, and usually they're the things we want the very most and cherish the most. No pain, no gain.

Turn Your Lemons Into Lemonade

Do you think you have problems? Let me tell you about somebody who really has problems.

Once you see Darrell you never forget him. When he was five years old, Darrell accidently lit the car on fire while his mom was in the grocery store. His face was terribly burned and the hot foam padding stuck to many parts of his body and melted his skin. He has no eyebrows or eyelashes, and he wears a wig to cover as much of his head as possible. The skin grafts are all folded and twisted, giving his face more the appearance of a mask than a human.

How do you feel about your problems now? Let me tell you some more about Darrell. He's forty now and has a job. He's had lots of jobs. He's responsible and even has a business of his own. Darrell never let the horrible scars of a childhood accident ruin his life. He made the best of a bad situation. Somehow Darrell even manages to see a bright spot to the accident: "I have two brothers" he said "and they are in prison now. We had a bad family life. I could have wound up in prison with a wasted life too, but I knew I couldn't hide behind my problems, I had to overcome them."

With an attitude like that, an ability to see the bright side, Darrell doesn't have problems. Don't hide behind your problems, overcome them. Turn your lemons into lemonade!

How Hard Do You Push Yourself?

How hard do you push yourself in life when there is something you want to improve? Do you ever push yourself to what you feel is your limit, to a point where it even causes you discomfort and pain?

I love to ski. Last year I was waiting in a lift line behind a fellow wearing a seven hundred dollar ski outfit. He was bragging about how he hadn't fallen all day, and sure enough the black and silver suit was spotless. In contrast, there I was, out of breath with snow hanging from my clothes. I was lucky to be alive! I decided to watch the guy take a run.

He traversed the hill back and forth, back and forth never attempting anything new and never taking a risk to become better. I saw him again the other day. A year had gone by, and again he was bragging he hadn't fallen all day. So I watched again, and sure enough there he skied, back and forth, just as he was doing the year before.

Sure, I fall more than this guy, but he never pushes himself to his limit. He never takes a chance on success. He hasn't improved one bit in over a year! Myself, I'll take a mountful of the clean white stuff and the humiliation of falling anytime if it will help me become better today than I was yesterday. Don't be afraid to fail! Don't be afraid to point your skis down the mountain of life and go for it! We all learned to walk step-fall-step.

Don't Feel Inferior

Feeling inferior is the worst, the absolute pits! Believe me, I know. I had a bad problem in high school, and it really gave me an inferiority complex. I had so many pimples the teacher sent me home one day for fear I had chicken pox. When I came back, I went to sleep in my math class and the kids played connect-the-dots on my face. Do you know the feeling?

I know about those days when you feel like a complete and total pine cone. You know, the feeling of no brains. When people look at you as if the line is busy, but nobody's on the phone.

I wasn't always the pride and joy of my parents, either. I swear there were times when my father was so embarrassed with me that he probably wished he could keep the picture that came with the wallet when he bought it.

Everyone, regardless of how beautiful, rich or famous they are, has something they don't like about themselves. And we all have bad experiences. So why do we let these complexes adversely affect our lives? Nobody's perfect. We are only human! If you're presently having some heartache, I know what you're going through. I wouldn't be telling you if I hadn't been there myself. So remember, bad experiences, like my pimples, eventually go away. Don't let what you don't have or can't do, get in the way of what you do have and can do. You're significant and important just the way you are! You are a child of the universe and you are supposed to be here!

The Worst Usually Never Happens

Did you ever look down the road and see something bad in the distance. It may be a police roadblock up ahead and you forgot to bring your license or your inspection sticker has expired. Maybe you have an exam coming up and you have forgotten to study and memorize the things you know you should. Or you have to give a speech or a report and you worry you won't even be able to remember your own name when it comes time to perform. Maybe there is an audition in the future, a try out for an athletic team.

Of course there is always the feeling we get when we sit in the dentist's waiting room. We know eventually the tooth is going to feel better, but in the meantime it's bad news.

Life is full of those horrible expectations. Unfortunately, we have a habit of blowing them all out of proportion. We can turn a scary little fantasy into a full fledged Frankenstein nightmare if we let our imaginations run wild. The truth is, the worst thing we expect usually never happens. This is what we call fear. Fear is worrying about the consequences of something bad happening when in reality it usually doesn't happen.

The only thing we have to fear is fear itself. Instead of worrying about what might happen, take care of what is happening.

You Can't Buy Happiness,
But You Can Find It

If you ask most people what they want the most from life, it would probably be either happiness or money. One thing is sure: It isn't always the people with the most money who have the most happiness. Happiness is sometimes overlooked because it doesn't cost anything. Here are some thoughts on happiness.

You can't pursue happiness and catch it. It comes to you unaware when you are helping others.

Happiness doesn't depend upon what happens outside of you but on what happens inside of you; it is measured by the way you meet the problems in your life.

Abe Lincoln said: "Happiness is a state of mind. We are as happy as we make up our minds to be."

Happiness grows out of harmonious relationships with others, based on good will, tolerance, understanding and love.

You don't feel happiness from doing easy work. You feel it from the achievement of a difficult task that demanded your best.

The secret to happiness is to meet each day believing you can deal with everything that comes your way.

No, you can't buy happiness, but you can find it. Decide today what will truly make you happy. Don't delay, pursue it.

Face Problems Don't Run From Them

Do you find yourself moaning about your problems? About the burdens and difficulties of life in general?

What's the matter with you? Did you think it was going to be easy? Nobody said it was going to be easy.

Life is sometimes difficult. It is a truth we must accept, and once we accept that fact and truly understand it — then life is no longer difficult.

You will always have problems. You have no choice. The choice is: Do you want to moan about them or solve them? Remember, the purpose of life is to become expert problem solvers.

Benjamin Franklin told us, "Those things that hurt, instruct." Knowing this, wise people actually welcome the pain of problems. On the other hand, if we have a tendency to avoid problems we are showing that we don't want to deal with reality. People who avoid problems and reality too much begin to suffer mental illness.

Don't be one who sidesteps and avoids problems, always looking for an easy way out. These individuals are in trouble and build fantasies which allow them to totally exclude reality. Drugs, alcohol, lies, stealing and other rebellious behavior are often a result of trying to avoid problems.

When we stop dealing with problems, we stop growing and begin to shrivel. Don't let the pain of problems force you to side step and dodge them. Learn to face them and solve them. Avoiding problems only makes it worse.

Dealing With Fear

There are situations we fear. We fear failing. We fear what others might think. We fear doctors, and we fear taking tests. The list is long.

What is fear? Fear is real. It won't just go away. It forces us to either deal with it or let it control us. To overcome fear, we must face it head on.

A friend of mine, Zig Ziglar, defines fear as "false evidence appearing real." Fear causes us to worry because it appears to us that something bad is going to happen, when in reality it never ever does.

Some people live, hoping to avoid fearful situations and not have to deal with them. Some avoid every situation which could possibly cause them fear. Overcoming what we fear is a necessary step to growth. Each time we overcome a fearful situation, we grow. Don't let fear hold you emotionally hostage. Deal with what scares you most by going ahead and doing it. Soon the fear will leave you.

Fully 40 percent of our worries never happen, 30 percent are in the past and cannot be changed, 12 percent are needless health worries, 10 percent are worries about general things, and only about 8 percent are real. The rest we create in our minds. Stop worrying and fearing the worst. Work to prepare yourself for accomplishment, and then expect the best.

Do The Worst Part First

Do you like cake? If you do, which part of the cake do you like better? The cake or the frosting?

Now consider how you eat cake when it is served. Do you attack the part of the cake you like most and save the least gratifying part for the last?

I'm not the Galloping Gourmet, and I'm not going to bake you a cake. I'm trying to get you to compare your study habits to eating cake. Do you do the easy part of your homework first and save the rest for later?

If you do, there is a word for that habit. It is called procrastination — putting things off we don't want to do because they're hard for us to do.

Next time you have an unpleasant task to accomplish, do it first. Force yourself to accomplish what you dread first. Don't save it for last. Get the pain over. Do the part of the job you are dreading right off the bat. Then you have the advantage of having your mind clear to do the things in life you enjoy. You get the worry over. It really is the only decent way to do anything. Play now, pay later is a bad motto to go through life with. Learn to delay gratification. Some things in life simply have to be done in order of importance, not in order of desire. Do what you should do when you should do it and be where you should be when you should be there. In life, eat the cake first and save the wonderful, easy chewing, best part of the cake – the frosting (the easy and most gratifying task) until last!

Dealing With Problems

Do you solve your problems or do you just kind of try and hope they go away?

The happiest individuals in life aren't those without any problems, they are the people who know how to solve their problems. Just like anything else in life there are right ways and wrong ways to solve problems.

First there is the banger. They practice the panic method. They get in their car and push the gas pedal before they know where they're going. They just start trying things without a plan, lashing out recklessly, hoping for a solution. They are nervous people who spend a lot of sleepless nights. Their problems seldom get solved.

The other kind of problem solver isn't a banger, but a thinker. Here's what they advise us to do.

1. Write your problem down on paper.

2. List the challenges keeping you from solving it.

3. List people you know and other sources which might be helpful in tackling the problem.

4. List all your possible courses of action.

5. Visualize the results of each course of action.

6. Choose the best course of action then pursue it. If it doesn't work and you've really tried, try another way.

Where there's a will there's a won't. Don't worry about the won't works. There's always a will work. Find it.

Champions Don't Feel Pressure

Champions aren't great all the time, but they are when they need to be. They understand their capacities and abilities, overcome obstacles, and rise to the occasion when they have to. That's why champions seldom buckle under pressure.

In fact, to a champion pressure doesn't exist. They know in the toughest moments they can do what they have to do. They understand pressure is not something that is naturally there. It is created in your mind when you begin to question your own ability. If you know what you can do, then there's never any question. You don't become tentative and wonder if you can do it. You know you can do it. At the critical moment of a match or a game, or a test or a business deal, you realize you've practiced enough before your performance to be ready for the situation which would scare you otherwise. Only self-doubt creates pressure.

A champion doesn't have to hold back in a crucial moment. Instead he can go for it, knowing he can do it because he's done it before. Instead of being cautious, a champion goes for "downtown." It's the only way his performance will be good enough to win.

I guess the message here is to practice hard to eliminate worry and overcome the problems before the performance. If you practice like you play, you'll play like you practice.

LEARNING

Only Perfect Practice Makes Perfect

During a school day there are probably times when you ask yourself, "What's the point; why learn this?"

The fact is, to learn something the right way from the start puts you way ahead of whoever learns the wrong way. There is an old saying that practice makes perfect. It isn't true!

Jack Nicklaus, the famous golfer, said practice doesn't do a person any good if the methods and principles he is repeating are wrong in the first place. This kind of practice only reinforces bad habits that will be even harder to break in the future. Only practicing the right golf swing will give you a perfect golf swing.

School is important because it teaches us the right way to practice so maximum learning can result. If a teacher had taught you in first grade the letter 'C' was an 'S,' you would have repeated it in your mind and it would have been wrong. But you aren't taught the wrong way to do things in school. Instead you are shown the right way to do things so you don't start out with bad habits.

Bad habits are hard to break. Learning the right way from the start is the best way to get it right your whole life. Any life that starts out that way can only get better. Remember, practice doesn't make perfect; perfect practice makes perfect.

Demographic Portrait of America

When the more than 3.6 million children entering kindergarten this fall graduate from school, the United States will be on the verge of the 21st century. What are the demographics of this generation? According to Harold Hodgkinson:

- One out of four children will be from families in poverty.
- One out of seven will be children of teenage mothers.
- 15% will be physically or mentally handicapped.
- 15% will be immigrants who speak a language other than English.
- One out of seven will be children of unmarried parents.
- 40% will live in a broken home before they reach the age of 18.
- Ten percent will have poorly educated or illiterate parents.
- Nearly one out of three will be latch key children.
- One out of four will not finish school.

These frightening statistics should not lead to despair, but rather new commitment and dedication to rise to the challenges ahead. We must put success into the curriculum and show these children that they can succeed despite their unfair circumstances.

Our nation's future depends on the education decisions made today.

Getting By Lately?

In school, are you cutting corners and just barely slipping through your classes? Do you do as little as possible, give as little as possible, or work as little as possible just to "get by?"

It's possible to make a minimum effort in a class and study as little as possible to acquire credit for the course and achieve a minimum passing grade. But if you do it in school you will do it in life! Young people often suppose there is time in the far future for all they want to get done. They figure that for now it's cool to just simply "get by" until something better comes along.

The days of this life are limited no matter how many you might think lay ahead of you! Stop cheating yourself! Everything you ever gain in life is going to depend on how much you put into it. We only grow by growing and only do by doing. Find out what you can do by really doing, not by just "getting by." Start doing your best today, before it gets too late in life. If you hold back on your best effort you're only cheating yourself. You aren't putting anything over on anybody but you.

Make an effort to find out what you can do instead of worrying about what you have to do. Anyone just "getting by," is getting behind.

Learning Is Not An 8 To 5 Job

How important is the process of learning? Each one of us would probably give a different answer to that question because learning is as important as you want to make it. It is a priority each one of us must set as individuals. You set your priorities in your life. You control the effort you put into learning.

When we attend school we sometimes have a tendency to see learning as just something which takes place from eight in the morning until three-thirty in the afternoon. We condition our minds to only be turned on between those hours Monday through Friday as we attend our classes. Learning is a lifelong process. You have to exercise your mind just as you exercise your body in order to strengthen it and get the most out of it.

Classically defined, learning is nothing more than the acquisition of knowledge or skill. Just because we receive good instruction doesn't mean we also master the knowledge or skill that goes with it. Instruction alone won't maximize your learning potential. Only through work and study on your own part will you ever master anything you are taught. Learning is not just an eight to five job. It's a lifelong process of hard work and practical application of instruction. Learning is a turn on, a turn on of the mind. Keep it turned on.

What Is Involved Evolves

Are you involved in activities at your school?

If you become involved, you evolve. The amount of effort you put into anything you do is determined by your involvement in it.

The worst thing you can do in school is not want to be there. With that attitude, you'll fall behind and start feeling the pressure of making it up. You won't participate in extracurricular activities. You might even bag the whole thing. Drop out.

To get the most out of school, decide to be involved at school. It is proven that the more you are involved in activities at school, the better your grades and performance will be. Almost 100 percent of the persons who drop out of school never participate in any of the extra activities available to them.

Research has shown activities and academics equal excellence in education. For example, athletic competition builds self-respect, self-esteem, self-confidence and the value of teamwork. Activities help sustain motivation!

Get involved in school. You'll evolve into a better person. It's a proven fact. Any talent you have can be finely-tuned and nourished in school. I challenge you to get everything out of your school experience that is available. Become the best you can possibly be.

Great Teachers
Can Find Hidden Potential

One of the greatest football coaches of all time was Vince Lombardi. During one practice session Lombardi singled out one big lineman and tore into him.

"Son, you're a lousy football player. You're not blocking, you're not putting out. It's over for you. Go take a shower." The big guard lumbered into the dressing room with his head down. Forty-five minutes later when Lombardi went to the locker room the player was sitting in front of his locker with his head down, weeping quietly.

Sensing his mood, Lombardi put his arm around his shoulder. "Son, I told you the truth. You are a lousy football player. However, in all fairness to you, I should have finished the story. Inside of you is a great football player, and I'm going to stick by your side until the great football player inside of you has a chance to come out."

Jerry Kramer felt better. In fact, he felt so much better he became an All-Pro lineman and was voted the best guard to play in the first fifty years of pro football.

Vince Lombardi saw things in men they seldom saw in themselves. He had an ability to inspire men to use the talent they had. Great teachers have the same ability to find in students their hidden potential. Listen to your teachers, and let them bring out the best in you. Show them you are genuinely interested in your eduction.

The State of Becoming

Your body makes one billion new red blood cells every day. Every few weeks your entire layer of outer skin is replaced. In an average lifetime, your head grows twenty-five feet of hair that you have to decide what to do with periodically.

Our bodies and our minds are both in a state of becoming. Are you becoming something besides older?

I remember a lesson my high-school English teacher taught me. He had our class write poems, and he called on me to read mine in class. I wished that poem in my hand would catch fire or maybe blow out the window, but it just sat there in my hand waiting to be read. I reluctantly started to read, but then had to stop.

"I can't do this. I'm no poet," I said.

The whole class went silent.

"Young man, don't you ever let me hear you say I can't again. Right now you don't know what you are and what you may become. You are still developing and being created. That's why we all are here in this class — to grow, to develop, to work at what we can become."

Let's appreciate our teachers. Good teachers are in your school to help you realize what you might become. Help them. Don't just say, "Teach me." Cooperate and say, "I'm here to learn."

Learn It Now; Apply It Later

Some days I'll bet you sit in the classroom and say, "What good is learning this stuff; I'll never use it."

You're right. If you don't learn it, you'll never get the chance to use it. Why not at least give yourself the option of having it in your mind in case you need it one day.

I played football, and thought math was a real drag. Why should I care about math when we never had to go past hut three on a signal count. During one math test I asked a guy on the team how far he was from the right answer, and he said about two seats away. I don't play football anymore, and I wish I knew more about math. You never know when something you learn might come in handy.

All knowledge is important. I guarantee you'll have a chance to use everything you learn. Some of those guys I played football with went on to get big professional contracts, and they have to pay some accountant to count their money because they blew off math class.

Once you are taught something, it's up to you to apply it in your life. Your challenge isn't to say what you do need and don't need to know to get through life. Your challenge is to learn, and look for ways to apply what you learn later. Don't worry; you'll get a chance. The only knowledge not worth having is knowledge which is never applied.

Books

Do you take time to read for your own enjoyment? Sure you read school work, but there are all kinds of adventures to be lived by reading. Everyone loves a great story. That's exactly what the best books do, tell stories. There are stories written on any subject you could name.

It's a priceless privilege to be able to live the greatest stories told by the world's greatest storytellers. Once you know how to read it isn't just an opportunity but an obligation to read what the great minds have written, and it's important to choose carefully what it is that you read.

Books are a lot like people, there are good ones and bad ones, depending on what's inside of them. The wrong kind of book is just like the wrong kind of person. Neither one of them is good to associate with, they both give you ideas and create situations which are potentially dangerous to you. And, like people, the potentially dangerous ones seem to be on the increase. Choosing the books you read is as important as choosing the friends you associate with. You spend time with both of them. They both give you ideas.

Of all the books you've read, what is your favorite? Remember how you couldn't wait to finish it? Ask someone you respect their opinion about what you should read? Read often to understand life and improve your understanding of words, issues, cultures, and yourself.

Learn It Now

I heard a good joke the other day but it happens to be in Korean. !&%#*&%$#*$#&%**$##

"Man isn't that the greatest joke? I almost die laughing every time I hear it. Why aren't you laughing? What's the matter with you? Have you already heard it?"

That's not a very pleasant feeling is it? Not being able to understand or not being understood are two of the most frustrating situations in life.

You'll feel that way your whole life if you don't learn to read and write while you're in school. It'll seem like everybody is using a different language and that you're not in on any of it.

Be honest with yourself. Are you having a problem writing what you want to say or reading what you want to read? If you are, ask a counselor for help. Don't live your life unable to write what you mean or read what you see.

Reward yourself and take the opportunity to learn to communicate. Most of us would not be able to understand a joke in Korean. But each of us can and should learn the language we are being taught. Are you doing your best to master the language you are supposed to be learning. If you don't feel comfortable with it for some reason, find out why. Discover what is holding you back. Don't let illiteracy play a joke on you. It's a joke that lasts a lifetime.

How To Pass Class

1. BRING THE TEACHER NEWSPAPER CLIPPINGS DEALING WITH THE SUBJECT. Demonstrates fiery interest and gives the teacher timely items to mention to the class. If you can't find clippings dealing with the subject, bring in any clippings at random. The teacher thinks everything deals with the subject.

2. LOOK ALERT. Take notes EAGERLY!! If you do look at your watch, don't stare at it unbelievingly and shake it.

3. NOD FREQUENTLY AND MURMUR, "HOW TRUE!!" To you this may seem exaggerated, but to the teacher it's quite objective.

4. SIT IN FRONT, NEAR THE TEACHER. (Applies only if you intend to stay awake.) If you are going to all the trouble of making a good impression, you might as well let the teacher know who you are, especially in a large class.

5. LAUGH AT THE TEACHER'S JOKES. You CAN tell when a joke is told if the teacher looks up from the notes and smiles expectantly.

6. ASK FOR OUTSIDE READING. (You don't have to read it. Just ask for it.)

7. IF YOU MUST SLEEP, ARRANGE TO BE AWAKENED AT THE END OF THE CLASS! It creates an unfavorable impression if the rest of the class has left and you sit there alone, still dozing.

8. BE SURE THE BOOK YOU ARE READING DURING THE CLASS LOOKS LIKE A BOOK FROM THE CLASS. If you do math in psychology class, or are trying to finish the latest hot novel, match the books for size and color.

9. ASK ANY QUESTIONS YOU THINK THAT THE TEACHER CAN ANSWER. Conversely, avoid announcing that you have found the answer to the question the teacher COULDN'T answer and in your younger brother's second grade reader.

10. CALL ATTENTION TO THE TEACHER'S WRITING. Produces an exquisitely pleasant experience connected with you. If you know the teacher has written a book or an article, ask about it in class.

GROWING UP

Look Hard Before You Leave Home

Some people run around their whole lives looking for what will make them happy when it's right under their feet. Some leave home and run away, looking for a better life than they have at home. The truth is, happiness might exist right where they are, in their own homes.

In the middle 1800's there was a gold rush in America. Before it ever officially started, one man sold his ranch in northern California to move to southern California to look for gold. He sold his home to a former army colonel and never came back. The colonel put a mill on a stream that ran through the property. One day his little girl brought home some sand from the stream in a jar, and she sifted through it. In the sand were the first shining nuggets of gold that were ever discovered in California.

The man who had owned the ranch wanted gold. If he had stayed on his land, he could have secured all the gold he ever needed. Since that day, thirty-eight million dollars of gold have been taken out of that land he sold.

It's better to try to make the most of what you have at home before trying to make it better by running away and moving somewhere else. Maybe what can really make you happy is just hidden from your sight temporarily, out of view for just a while. Look hard before you leave. Dig where you are before you sell!

I Don't Know What To Do

I talk a lot about what you have to do to be a success. I tell you how to get what you want from life. I talk about people who work toward what they want to be, and how they make their dreams come true.

But you say to yourself, I don't know what I want to do. That's normal. A lot of people, especially males, haven't decided what they want to do with their lives. Nobody is telling you you have to make a decision today, as long as you understand that eventually you'll have to start working toward doing something with your life. In the meantime, the general knowledge you get in life gives you a great background for making that choice. Going to school, for instance, gives you a chance to build good work habits while you are waiting to make the decision on your future. Keep hanging in there, but while you do, give everything you do your very best shot. Learn how to work.

Making the decision about what you want is the hard part. Once you know that — once you have that purpose — you'll be well practiced at giving your maximum effort. You'll know the steps to take toward getting what you want. Until you start to feel that purpose, that desire to commit to something and enjoy the fulfillment of working toward it, spend your time learning to listen, read, implement, evaluate, and revise so when the time comes you'll be ready.

Growing Up Is Tough

The other day I saw a father yelling the typical things parents yell at fourteen-year-old sons. You know the kinds of things I'm talking about: "Won't you ever learn?" "You're impossible." And finally, the one all kids hear: "Why don't you grow up?"

This fourteen-year-old had an interesting reply to his father's question: "That's what I'm trying to do."

I guess that's what all young people are trying to do — grow up. It isn't an easy job! Sometimes our parents make us feel like fools, and we almost resent them for treating us like we don't know what we're doing.

That's what's so tough about being a teenager. You aren't a kid anymore, but you aren't sure what being an adult is all about. You have an idea, but you aren't sure you'll measure up to it or that you want to leave behind the joy of being a kid.

How many of us, when we're sixteen wish we were twenty-one? All of us go through it! But remember growing up takes time. It shouldn't happen overnight or at the same age for everybody. Don't put pressure on yourself to be an adult before you're ready. Growing up means you will accept personal responsibility for your own actions, and all anyone expects you to do is to try your best and do it little by little. You have the rest of your life to be an adult. So don't grow up too fast! Make the transition in the way you feel comfortable.

Its Not A Way Out

A lot of discussion has taken place recently about what happens to us after we die. Numerous accounts have been given of people who have actually suffered death, only to come back and tell about what they went through during the moments they were dead and had left their bodies. (Books like "Return from Tomorrow").

This isn't a ghost story, but it's leading to a serious consideration anybody should make who might be thinking about taking his or her own life. Many of these accounts which have been related have been related by suicide attempts. I'm talking honestly and candidly here because I don't want anybody to make the mistake of taking his or her own life. It would be the biggest mistake of your life. The reasons are frightening.

From what information has been gathered, those who have attempted suicide have clearly seen that their anguish is not ended. Rather, the anguish is compounded and multiplied as they desire to apologize to their loved ones for what they did. But the problem is they can't. They follow their relatives around trying to apologize, but they can't be heard. Killing themselves hasn't helped a thing, only made things worse. They beg for a chance to come back and solve their problems. They desperately want another chance to face their challenges head-on with courage. Give yourself another chance. Any problem can and must be overcome. Where there's a will, there is always a way! We have to deal with life in life and deal with death at death. Suicide is not the answer! Anybody can hang in there long enough to take one more step! Never, ever quit!!

I Never Thought They'd Do It

Do you know anyone talking about taking his or her own life? If so, it is probably very hard for that person to talk to you about it. The individual probably feels ashamed. Therefore, listen to him or her and always take them serious! Show concern and ask questions directly. Find out how serious the person is and what prompted it. Ask if your friend has talked to anyone else about it. See if he has decided how he would do it. Then ask if your friend would like to talk about it with someone with more expertise. Keep the lines of communication open. You might be the last hope. Let your friend get all his or her feelings out. Then get help!

Don't refuse to talk to your friend. It would only reinforce his fear that you and others find the idea repulsive. Don't be afraid to talk about it. Don't tell him how good he has it and how stupid he is. It only makes him feel more worthless and hopeless.

Your efforts in helping the suicidal person get help might save a life. People have a will to live that can be regained. Anyone can find a full, productive, meaningful, happy life again. You are the first vital link in helping that person to feel better about himself of herself. Don't be the one who says: "I didn't take him seriously" or "I never thought she'd do it." If you really love the person, get them professional counseling and keep your friendship alive!

ALCOHOL & DRUGS

They Ought To Rent Beer Not Sell It

They ought to rent beer not sell it!

Anyone who drinks beer knows how long it stays with you. You go to the store, pay four bucks for a six pack, drink it down and spend the rest of the night looking for a restroom. For the amount of time it stays in you, the money you lay out could be spent in a lot smarter ways.

Just think of it, if you have a party and spend money for ten six packs of beer, you've gone through fifty bucks. All you have to show for it is maybe seven trips to the rest room. The beer is floating down a sewer somewhere, your money is gone, your time is wasted, and worst of all if you try to drive home you'll probably kill yourself and others. A lot of time is wasted and a lot of lives are lost by people sitting around drinking beer. And what good does alcohol do?

Alcohol has driven people to suicide and ruined friendships and marriages — and still people want to spend hard-earned money on alcohol. I know alcohol never solved any problems for anybody, but it sure causes a few! I'm no square, but I know a good investment when I see it. Beer is not a good investment. Alcohol, period, is not a wise investment! People should just find something else to spend their money on. There has to be better ways to squander hard earned cash. As hard as it is to get, you had better make it last. Drinking alcohol is only good for one thing — wasting a life.

A Word of Wisdom

John ordered one more fast one. He was careful about his drinking because his wife Melba worried. She said liquor made him too confident and not cautious enough. John laughed, women never really understand their men he thought. Instead they always worry about things that never happen. He snapped up the shot glass, tilted his head and nodded to the bartender as he left.

Outside, he patted his car, put on his gloves in the winter air and thought about how happy he was. He owned a house and only eight months earlier he and Melba had had a son, now she was pregnant again, a girl he hoped.

John was hurrying to pick up Melba at the doctor's office. The car slid on the icy roads but he had to hurry because he had stopped at the bar. He speeded up a notch. Suddenly, he realized he wouldn't be able to make the turn at the bottom of the hill. He was going way too fast! The car was going to go through the guard rail and into the water. He propped his door open with his foot so he could get out when it hit the water. He planned to push the door open and swim to the bank.

People saw the old car coming and watched as it splashed into the water. As he planned, John got out safely and swam for shore. People cheered when he arrived safely. He thought, "See, I can handle my liquor." Then John remembered he had left his little son Jared in the car seat in the back. The car sunk.

Never drink and drive!

Drunk-Driving is Everyone's Business

It's nobody's business what I drink!
I care not what the neighbors think.
Or how many laws they choose to pass!
I'll tell the world I'll have my glass!
Here's one man's freedom that cannot be curbed,
My right to drink is undisturbed.

So he drank in spite of law or man,
Then got into his old tin can:
Stepped on the gas and let it go,
Down the highway to and fro.
He took the curves at fifty miles
With bleary eyes and drunken smiles.

Not long till a car he tried to pass;
There was a crash, a scream and breaking glass.
The other car was upside down,
About two miles from the nearest town.

The man was clear but his wife was caught,
And she needed help of that drunken sot,
Who sat in a maudlin, drunken daze,
And heard the scream and saw the blaze,
But was too far gone to save a life,
By lifting the car from off his wife.

The car was burned, and the mother died,
While a husband wept and baby cried,
And a drunk sat by — and still some think
It's nobodys business what they drink!

Tonight, if you decide to drink and drive, before you leave
home, make sure you kiss your mother goodbye!

An Eye Opener

The Drunkard's Child . . .

My father is a drunkard,
My mother she is dead,
And I am just an orphan child —
No place to lay my head.
All through this world I wander,
They drive me from their door;
Some day I'll find a welcome
On Heaven's golden shore.
Now, if to me you'll listen,
I'll tell you a story sad
How drinking rum and the gambling "hell,"
Has stole away my dad.
My mother is in Heaven
Where God and the Angels smile,
And now I know she's watching
Her lonely orphan child.
We all were once so happy.
And had a happy home,
Till dad he went to drinking rum,
And then he gambled some.
He left my darling mother.
She died of a broken heart;
And as I tell my story,
I see your tear drops start.
Don't weep for me and mother.
Although I know it's sad,
But try and get some one to cheer
And save poor lonely dad.
I'm awful cold and hungry —
He closed his eyes and sighed,
And those who heard his story
Knew the orphan child had died!

— *Author Unknown*

The Dumb Things We Do When We Drive

What are some of the dumb things that happen while you drive your car?

Have you ever stopped at a light and felt you were just a little bit too far into the intersection, so you back up a little just for safety. And when the light changes, you give it some gas, only to realize you are still in reverse and on top of the guy's bumper behind you?

Have you ever followed a car that had it's left hand blinker on for over five miles and every time you go to pass you think, "no, this may be it?"

Have you ever noticed that everyone going slower than you you call an idiot, and everyone who passes you you call a maniac?

No doubt about it, when we drive we do some dumb things. There's one dumb thing you should never do when you drive. Each year 50,000 people are killed and two million are seriously injured as a result of drunk driving. Eighty percent of first accidents are fatal accidents. That means you don't get two chances. Your first mistake is your last mistake.

It's a mistake to ever drive when you drink or drive under the influence of drugs. When I was in high school, many of my friends were killed as a result of drunk driving — seventeen-year-old guys with so much to live for.

When we drive, we do enough dumb things on our own without compounding the problem. If you drink, don't drive. The life you save might be your own or someone else's son or daughter, or best friend.

Drinking Is Scary

What is so scary about drinking?

Ask Frank. When Frank was in high school, he was president of his freshman and senior classes. He was handsome and popular, played basketball and was an expert in woodshop. Frank is forty now, and he's dying — but not from cancer or heart disease.

Frank is an alcoholic who has ruined his liver from drinking. It is so diseased it bulges out on one side of his body. Frank is scared, but not of dying. He is scared of running out of alcohol. When alcoholics run out of alcohol, they have seizures, imagine distorted faces chasing them, see snakes and bugs crawling out of bottles.

Frank has been forced to drink anything with alcohol in it — shaving lotion, rubbing alcohol, cooking fuel — just to fight off his body's need for alcohol.

Instead of having a career and a family, his living consists of selling cookies he receives at shelters and rescue missions. With the money he makes selling the cookies, he and four other men can afford a bottle of wine to share together and keep alcohol in their blood so they don't get sick.

Are you scared yet, or do you want to hear more? Frank took his first drink in high school and said to himself, "This can't possibly hurt anybody." Frank was wrong.

Some Things Never Change

Kids today are smoking some funny cigarettes. You know, the kind of cigarettes you roll yourself and that give off a funny, sweet smell.

Those kind of cigarettes have been around for a while. I remember what they were calling those cigarettes when I was in high school and college. They called it dope. I never could figure out if they called it that because of the way it made you feel when you smoke it — the slurred speech, the red eyes — or if they called it dope because the only persons who smoked it or used it were dopes.

It was kind of new stuff when I was young. Now they know more about it. The stuff is poison. They have already found smoking the stuff ruins the ability of your mind to learn, and it takes away your ambition and desire to become something in your life. If you smoke a lot of it, it might even ruin your chances of ever having healthy children, or deprive you of the dreams you could have made come true.

Going on the assumption that the really important things in life are learning, achieving, and having a family, why would anyone want to use any product that promised to ruin their ability to do any of those things?

Yeah, when I was growing up, they were calling it dope. Some things never change. Anybody who smokes dope is still a dope. If you use it, stop. If you don't use it, don't get started. It's slow suicide!

Don't Do It

We all have an idol in high school, someone we want to be like. My friend Charlie had an idol named John.

John was a handsome, popular student-athlete Charlie wanted to emulate. One night John asked Charlie to a party. When Charlie arrived an ambulance was at the party with people crowded around it. Charlie fought through the crowd to see what was going down. John was in the ambulance writhing and screaming out of control.

John had just won a track scholarship to the University of California. Until that party, John was clean-cut and straight, an all-American guy who never messed with drugs. But earlier in the night some of his friends had talked him into taking some angel dust, PCP, one of the most deadly drugs going around the country. John had refused at first but after continual peer pressure and being called chicken and stuck-up, he smoked the joint.

John had a few laughs for a minute but they were the last laughs of joy he ever had. He suffered severe brain damage. He lost his scholarship and to this day he doesn't recognize his family or the so-called friends who dared him to try the drugs. They can't and won't help him now. John is in a mental institution for life!

People who sell you drugs only take your money, they won't help you when something goes wrong. I challenge you to find a real friend — someone who really cares about you — who will help you become the best you can be by getting high off life!

SERVICE

Be Not Weary

Sally thought she saw life change for the better when a man, a widower from her past, returned with a proposal of marriage. In his nice suit of clothes he talked of a prosperous farm. The prospects of a better life grew, for she understood him to mention servants, and that meant that he must be a man of substance. She accepted and crossed the river with him to view her new possessions: only to find a farm grown up to wild blackberry vines and a floorless, windowless hut; the only servants were two, thinly clad, barefoot children. She soon discovered that the father had borrowed the suit and boots he went a-courtin in.

Her first thought was obvious — go back home! But she looked at the children, especially the younger, a boy, whose melancholy gaze met hers.

For a moment she paused, then rolling up her sleeves she quietly spoke immortal words which ought to be engraven on every leader or teacher's heart, "I'll stay, for the sake of this boy."

Who among us today never feels frustration or discouragement? Has anyone ever taught youth without those moments which cry for and almost demand a release from the teaching assignment?

Never despair. The only thing God has to make a man out of is a boy, and you have him in your care while he's teachable. Who among us is wise enough to recognize a leader, president or world-record holder at 8, 10, or 12 years of age.

And Sally Bush didn't know when she looked at that melancholy face of ten years that her step-son would someday save his nation and become the immortal Abraham Lincoln.

Stay for the sake of a boy — Be not weary.

Count The Windows In Your World

Do you know anybody who concentrates only on their own well-being without any concern for others?

If you do, you know a selfish person. They are only aware of themselves. Why? Because they live in a mirror world. They have no windows. Henry Emerson Fosdick explains the mirror world some people live in.

The great day comes when a man begins to get himself off his hands. He has lived with a mind surrounded by mirrors. Every way he turned he saw himself. Now, however some of the mirrors have changed to windows. He can see through them to objective outlooks that challenge his interests. He begins to get out of himself, no longer the prisoner of self-reflections, but a free man in a world where persons, causes, truths and values exist for their own sakes. Thus, to pass from a mirror-mind to a mind with windows is an essential step in the development of real personality. Without it, no one ever achieves a meaningful life. No one ever gets off his hands and uses them.

No one would be happy if they were shut up in a room surrounded by mirrors. That selfish existence would be miserable. Maturity begins when you start turning those mirrors and thoughts into windows which help you become aware of the rest of the world. Only then will you understand the importance of service. Look beyond your own personal needs and become aware of the needs of others. Then serve!

IMPORTANT POETRY

The Best Way To Play Any Game

The best way to play any game in life is to give it your best. A lot of people have missed being the best they can be just because they didn't give their best to the end. So, whenever you play a game or commit to a project try and remember these words:

Whatever the game, and whatever the odds,
The winning is all up to you;
For it isn't the score, and it isn't the prize,
That counts when the playing is through!
In the great game of Life, it's the purpose to win,
And the courage to fight to the end.
That determines for you what degree of success
Will be scored to your credit, my friend.
The best you can do may not be quite enough
To defeat your opponents today;
But you never can lose, and you never can fail,
If you "put all you've got" in your play;
And the greatest reward that your efforts can bring,
Is the fact that you stood to the test —
That you played a clean game, and fought a good fight,
And you always were doing your best!

Anyone who gives their best, never really loses.

Does It Show In Your Face?

The next time you take a close look at yourself in the mirror, don't look at how your face looks, look at what it shows. Is there happiness on your face?

You don't have to tell how you live each day
You don't have to say if you work or play
A tried, true barometer serves in this place
However you live, it will show in your face
The false, the deceit that you bear in your heart
Will not stay inside when it first gets a start
For sinew and blood are a thin veil of lace
What you wear in your heart you wear on your face.
If your life is unselfish, if for others you live
For not what you get, but how much you give
If you live close to God in His infinite grace
You don't have to tell it, it shows in your face.

If there isn't happiness showing in your face, seek it out. Sometimes happiness isn't always doing what you want to do; it's doing what you don't want to do, and being glad you did it. It isn't only found by always doing what one likes, but in liking what one has to do.

Keep in mind that no one has ever injured their eyesight by looking on the bright side of things.

How Bad Do You Want It?

If you want a thing bad enough,
To go out and fight for it,
Work day and night for it,
Give up your time and your peace and your sleep for it,
If only the desire of it,
Makes you mad enough,
Never to tire of it,
Makes you hold all things tawdry and cheap for it,
If life seems all empty and useless without it,
And all that you scheme and dream is about it,
If you'll gladly sweat for it,
Fret for it,
Plan for it,
Lose all terror of God and man for it,
If you'll simply go after the thing that you want,
With all your capacity,
Strength and tenacity,
Faith, hope and confidence stern pertinacity,
If neither cold, poverty, famished and haunt,
Nor sickness, nor pain
Of body, or brain,
Can turn you away from the thing that you want,
If dogged and grim you besiege and beset it,
You'll get it.

Do As I Say Not As I Do

Do you know any individuals who say one thing then do another? If you do you can understand the importance of teaching by example. No one takes an individual too seriously who shows no consistency between what they say and what they do. Here's a poem with a message for all of us who sometimes say "do as I say, not as I do."

I'd rather see a sermon preached than hear one any day;
I'd rather someone walk with me than merely point the way.
The eye's a better pupil, and more willing than the ear;
Fine counsel is confusing, but examples always clear;
The finest of preachers are the men who live their creeds,
For to see good put into action, is what everybody needs.
I can learn to do it, if you'll let me see it done;
Your hand I see in action, your tongue too fast may run.
And the lecture you deliver may be very well and true,
But I'd rather get my lesson by observing what you do;
For I might misunderstand you, the high advice you give,
But, there's no misunderstanding how you act and how you live.

People believe what they see not what they hear. Think as much about how you are acting as you do about what you are saying. The whole world is watching, deciding what you are by the way you act and live.

Perseverance

Two frogs fell in a bowl of cream.
One had an optimistic gleam,
But the other took the gloomy view.
"We'll drown," he cried, and without adieu
He gave a last despairing cry,
Flung up his legs and said goodbye.
Said the other frog with a steady grin,
"I can't get out, but I won't give in;
I'll just swim around till my strength is spent,
Then will I die the more content."
Bravely he swam till it would seem
His struggles began to churn the cream.
On top of the butter at last he stopped,
And out of the bowl he gaily hopped.
What of the moral? It's easily found:
If you can't get out, keep swimming around.

The Teacher
I
The Pains

There's a time for every teacher
When the class has gone to pot,
And you feel that you are ready
Just to chuck the bloomin' lot;

When the lesson plan is futile
And you've spoken pretty blunt
To the kid that did a number
On your car that's parked out front;

Or a parent in a lather
Has spent time upon the phone
Making gross insinuations
In a most insulting tone;

When your talents go unnoticed,
And your salary's less than nice
While you find yourself a-scratchin'
From somebody else's lice;

Then you wonder why you wanted
To become a teaching fool,
And you know there's something better
Than just teaching in a school.

© — John W. Crawford

The Teacher
II
The Joys

But, there's joy around the corner
That can make it all worth while
When a child has learned his lesson
And can face you with a smile;

Or a parent says she's noticed
Quite a change in little Sal,
And that little monster Billy
Has become his daddy's pal;

And when Rob and Bob and Rudy,
Who can never do it right,
Are the stars within your classroom
On the "back to basics" night;

Or the shy one in the corner
Who has never said a word
Brings some flowers from his garden
For the teacher who's preferred;

Then your job brings great contentment
And you do it with a smile
Cause you really are a TEACHER
Who has gone that extra mile.

© — John W. Crawford

The Oyster

There once was an oyster, whose story I tell
Who found that some sand had got under his shell;
Just one little grain, but it gave him a pain
For oysters have feelings for all sorts of things.

How did he berate the working of fate
Which had led him to such a deplorable state?
Did he curse the government and cry for an election?
And cry that the seas should have given protection?

No. – He said to himself as he lay on the shelf,
Since I cannot remove it, I'll try to improve it.

The years rolled around as years always do.
And he came to his ultimate destiny — Stew!
And the small grain of sand that had bothered him so
Was a beautiful pearl, all richly aglow.

The tale has a moral, for isn't it grand
What an oyster can do with a morsel of sand?
What couldn't we do if we'd only begin
With all the things that get under our skin!!

Work Will Win When
Wishy-Washy Wishing Won't

Said the big white rooster, "Gosh all hemlock; things are really tough,
Seems that worms are getting scarcer and I cannot find enough;
What's become of all those fat ones is a mystery to me;
There were thousands through the rosy spell but now where can they be?"

The little red hen who heard him didn't grumble or complain,
She had gone through lots of dry spells, she had lived through
        floods of rain;
So she flew up on the grindstone and she gave her claws a whet,
As she said: "I've never seen the time there were no worms to get."

She picked a new and undug spot — the earth was hard and firm,
The big white rooster jeered, "New ground! That's no place for a worm."
The little red hen just spread her feet, she dug both fast and free,
"I must go to the worms," she said, "the worms won't come to me."

The rooster vainly spent his day, through habit, by the ways
Where fat worms have passed in squads, back in the rainy days.
When nightfall found him supperless, he growled in accents rough,
"I'm hungry as a fowl can be — conditions sure are tough."

He turned then to the little red hen and said, "It's worse with you,
For you're not only hungry but you must be tired, too.
I rested while I watched for worms so I feel fairly perk,
But how are you? Without worms, too? And after all that work."

The little red hen hopped to her perch and dropped her eyes to sleep,
And murmured in a drowsy tone, "Young man, hear this and weep,
I'm full of worms and happy, for I've dined both long and well,
The worms are there as always — but I had to dig like heck."

Reality

I destroyed the world last night.
The climactic point in an endless fight.
I blew the planet out of my sight —
While playing a video game.

But what do these men in our capitol mean
By building the ultimate killing machine?
And satellite war, hey now, that's <u>really</u> keen!
Can America keep its good name?

I wonder — Has Ron played Atari® today?
Is it worth a new quarter to learn not to slay?
Could we spend our defense budget better that way?
Don't they see — any war is the same?

War isn't a many splendored thing,
But on Armed Forces Day people shout, hum and sing
As parades of our weapons proclaim themselves king!
Who will tell them it isn't a game?

                                        —Mark C. Torrance

A Summer's Love

There will soon be
A nice summer's breeze
With plenty of sun
Shining through the trees
But as the sun goes down
And day turns to dark
The most you will see
Is lovers in the park
There will be lots of happiness
Floating in the air
With lovers holding hands
To be seen everywhere
This is how
The summer will be
Just wait a while longer
And you will see
The flowers will grow
Until they're in full bloom
The birds will be in trees
Singing their sweet tunes
The flowers will leave the scent
Of freshness in the air
The birds will be leaving
Sweet tunes everywhere
Your lady will leave you
To go out of town
She will not have a thought
Of fooling around
But when she needs you
To hold her in your arms
Some male will get her
By using his charms
Take it from me
For I lost my love
To someone I never imagined
A summer's love

Take Your Eyes Off the Ground

My gaze was cast upon the ground,
And with a critical eye
I saw each particle of dirt
And then said with a sigh,

"Lord, why must I put up with this?
It just does not seem fair,
For I've got so much to worry about
And, oh, so many cares."

The answer came back very faint;
I strained my ears to hear.
"Oh, what's He trying to say to me?
I wish that He were near."

I soon began to understand.
"Look upward!" was His plea.
"I cannot help you while your eyes
are down and not on Me!"

I slowly raised my drooping head
And was startled by the view,
For all things now were beautiful
All things had become new.

The voice came back so clearly now:
"You see it's up to you.
There's so much you've been blessed with
You must keep that in view.

That happiness, that peace of mind,
That joy you never found
Are always there if you'll but take
Your eyes up off the ground."

Activity

Are you an active member
the kind thats liked so well
OR are you just contented
With the button on your lapel?

Do you attend the meetings
and mingle with the flock.
Or do you stay at home,
And criticize and knock?

Do you take an active part,
To help the work along,
Or are you satisfied to be
The kind that just belong?

Do you push the crowd along
and make things really tick
or leave the work for just a few
And talk about the click?

Come to the meetings often
And help with hand and heart
Don't be just a member
But take an active part.

Think this over carefully
You know right from wrong
Are you an active member
Or do you just belong?

The Night Before Christmas
(A three page story)

Twas the night before Christmas
And all through the house
Things were real mellow . . . .
Even Irving, the mouse.

Our boots were hung up,
The incense was lit,
In hope that St. Nick
Would soon do his bit.

The tree was decked out,
It was really a sight,
With love beads and flowers
And a flashing strobe light.

Wearing my T-shirt
From Woodstock nation,
I was just getting into some
Good Meditation.

And my chick was doing
Some yoga in bed
Munching a fruit cake,
While propped on her head.

Then . . . Pow . . . In the light . . .
. . . A hullabaloo
It shook the waterbed
And woke up ol' Blue.
I stumbled around
And tripped on my beard.
It stuck to my toes
And really felt weird.

When I got to the window,
I was really uptight,
Cause the scene I perceived
Was a mind blowing sight!
What through my shades
Did I see through the snow?
But eight tiny mooses
And a wild U. F. O.

(continued on next page)

With this hip dude inside
Looking kinky and groovy . . .
I flashed . ."If this ain't Nick,
Must be the late movie" . . .

They blew in from the cosmos
Like some far out caboose
And this fat cat kept yelling
At each midget moose.
"Right on Dasher! On Dancer!
Rudolf be mean!
Get your bod's in high gear now,
And move this machine!"

Then onto the roof
They flew with a shout,
The whole kosmic crew
Really freaked me out!
They caused such a hassle
And made such a fuss,
I thought someone would call
The fuzz down on us . . .
But before I could say, "Cool it!"
"Hold down that loud jive,"
Nick zapped toward the chimney
And leaped in with a dive!

As he trucked from the fireplace,
His smile all a gleam,
I thought, "It's unreal, it must be a dream"
Then he nodded and said,
"This isn't a bummer . . .
Like, I've come in peace,
To groove my Yule number."

His duds were all fur,
Trimmed in leather and such,
And he came in stone funky . . .
He was really too much.
His back-pack was painted,
With black-light festoon,
Full of albums and posters,
And a neon balloon.

(continued on next page)

His eyes, a light show!
His beard, did-glow bright!
A plastic, fantastic, kaleidoscope sight!
He looked like a guru,
This beautiful cat . . .
I thought, like wow!
This dude knows where it's at!

"Don't want to sound heavy,"
He said with a grin,
"My message is simple,
So dig it, tune in."
"I brought you some goodies,
But that not's the thing.
My real trip is bringing,
Good vibes to this scene."

So we rapped 'til dawn,
About peace, love and truth,
Then he said, "Gotta split now,
Or I'll be late in Duluth."
He wiggled his nose and said,
"I did my bit."
And straight up the smoke hole,
This fat cat did split!

As he spun from the roof,
And into the air.
He shouted, "Let's get it together,
All you people down there!
Merry Christmas to all,
And to all a good night!"
And then in a flash,
He streaked out of sight.
                    (really out of sight)

The Touch of the Master's Hand

'Twas battered and scarred, and the auctioneer
Thought it scarcely worth his while
To waste much time on the old violin,
But held it up with a smile.

"What am I bid, good folk," he cried,
"Who'll start bidding for me?
A dollar, a dollar — now two, only two —
Two dollars, and who'll make it three?"

"Three dollars once, three dollars twice.
Going for three" — but no!
From the room far back a gray-haired man
Came forward and picked up the bow;

Then wiping the dust from the old violin,
And tightening up the strings,
He played a melody pure and sweet,
As sweet as an angel sings.

The music ceased and the auctioneer
With a voice that was quiet and low,
Said: "What am I bid for the old violin?"
And he held it up with the bow.

"A thousand dollars — and who'll make it two
Two thousand — and who'll make it three?
Three thousand once — three thousand twice —
And going — and gone," said he.

The people cheered, but some of them cried,
"We do not quite understand —
What changed its worth?" The man replied,
"The touch of the Master's hand."

And many a man with life out of tune
And battered and torn with sin.
Is auctioned cheap to the thoughtless crowd,
Much like the old violin.

A "mess of pottage," a glass of wine
A game — and he travels on.
He's going once, and going twice,
He's going — and almost gone!

But the master comes, and the foolish crowd
Never can quite understand
The worth of a soul, and the change that's wrought
By the touch of the Master's hand.

229

If

If you can keep your head when all about you are losing theirs and
   blaming it on you,
If you can trust yourself when all men doubt you but make allowance
   for their doubting too;
If you can wait and not be tired by waiting, or being lied about, don't
   deal in lies,
Or being hated, don't give way to hating and yet don't look too good,
   not talk too wise.

If you can dream – and not make dreams your master; if you can think
   and not make thoughts your aim,
If you can meet with triumph and disaster and treat those two imposters
   just the same;
If you can bear to hear the truth you've spoken twisted by knaves to
   make a trap for fools
Or watch the things you gave your life to, broken, and stoop and build
   'em up again with worn out tools.

If you can make one heap of all your winnings and risk it on one turn
   of pitch and toss,
And lose, and start again at your beginning and never breathe a word
   about your loss;
If you can force your heart and nerve and sinew to serve your turn
   long after they are gone
And so hold on when there is nothing in you except the will which
   says to them "Hold on!"

If you can talk with crowds and keep your virtue or walk with Kings –
   nor lose the common touch,
If neither foes nor loving friends can hurt you, if all men count with
   you, but none too much;
If you can fill the unforgiving minute with sixty seconds' worth of
   distance run,
Yours is the earth and everything that's in it, and – what is more –
   You'll be a man, my son.

— Rudyard Kipling

The Optimist Creed

AN OPTIMIST IS A PERSON WHO GOES FISHING FOR
WHALES WITH NOTHING BUT A ROW BOAT, A FISH-
ING ROD, AND A GALLON OF TARTAR SAUCE.

Promise Yourself

To be so strong that nothing can destroy your peace of mind.

To talk health, happiness, and prosperity to every person
you meet.

To make all your friends feel that there is something special
in them.

To look at the sunny side of everything and make your
optimism come true.

To think only of the best, to work only for the best and
expect only the best.

To be just as enthusiastic about the success of others as you
are about your own.

To forget the mistakes of the past and press on to the greater
achievements of the future.

To wear a cheerful countenance at all times and give every
living creature you meet a smile.

To give so much time to the improvement of yourself that
you have no time to criticize others.

To be too large for worry, too noble for anger, too strong
for fear, and too happy to permit the presence of trouble.

Christian D. Larson

Just Like His Dad

(Apply this also to relationships between big and little brothers
and to those who have others look to them for leadership.)

He wants to be like his dad you men,
    Did you ever think as you pause
That the boy who watches your every move
    Is building a set of laws?

He's molding a life you're the model for
    And whether it's good or bad
Depends on the kind of example set
    To the boy who'd be like his dad.

Would you have him go everywhere you go?
    Have him do just the things you do?
And see everything that your eyes behold
    And woo all the Gods you woo.

When you see the worship that shines in the eyes.
    of your loveable little lad
Would you rest content if he gets his wish
    And grows up to be just like his dad?

Desiderata

Go placidly amid the noise and haste and remember what peace there may be in silence. As far as possible without surrender be on good terms with all persons. Speak your truth quietly and clearly; and listen to others, even the dull and ignorant, they too have their story.

Avoid loud and aggressive persons, they are vexations to the spirit. If you compare yourself with others, you may become vain and bitter; for always there will be greater and lesser persons than yourself. Enjoy your achievements as well as your plans.

Keep interested in your own career, however humble; it is a real possession in the changing fortunes of time. Exercise caution in your business affairs; for the world is full of trickery. But let this not blind you to what virtue there is; many persons strive for high ideals; and everywhere life is full of heroism.

Be yourself. Especially, do not feign affection. Neither be cynical about love; for in the face of all aridity and disenchantment it is perennial as the grass.

Take kindly the counsel of the years, gracefully surrendering the things of youth. Nurture strength of spirit to shield you in sudden misfortune. But do not distress yourself with imaginings. Many fears are born of fatigue and loneliness. Beyond a wholesome discipline, be gentle with yourself.

You are a child of the universe, no less than the trees and the stars; and have a right to be here. And whether or not it is clear to you, no doubt the universe is unfolding as it should.

Therefore, be at peace with God, whatever you conceive Him to be, and whatever your labors and aspirations, in the noisy confusion of life keep peace with your soul.

With all its shame, drudgery and broken dreams, it is still a beautiful world. Be careful. Strive to be happy.

My Friend

I love you not only for what you are, but for what I am when I am with you. I love you not only for what you have made of yourself, but for what you are making of me. I love you for the part of me that you bring out. I love you for putting your hand into my heaped-up heart and passing over all the foolish and frivolous and weak things that you can't help but dimly see there, and for drawing out into the light all of the beautiful, radiant belongings that no one else had looked far enough to find.

I love you for ignoring the possibilities of the fool and the weakling in me, and for laying firm hold on the possibilities of the good in me. I love you for closing your eyes to the dischords in me, and for adding to the music in me by worshipful listening. I love you because you are helping me to make of the lumber of my life not a tavern, but a temple, and of the word of my every day not a reproach, but a song.

I love you because you have done more than any creed could have done to make me good, and more than any fate could have done to make me happy. You have done it without a touch, without a word, without a song. You have done it just by being yourself.

CONCLUSION

The Greatest Principle in Practice

In a highly emotional scene from the love story "THE WAY WE WERE" Barbra Streisand says to Robert Redford, "People are their principles."

It's true. In this book we've taken a look at a lot of principles and beliefs people have put into practice. We are all "Principles in Practice" every day of our lives. Our lives are guided by the principles we believe in. They determine whether we soar with the eagles, or are shackled by bad habits, scared to fly and mingle with the turkeys.

As we are our principles, life is a school of hard knocks. There are a lot of people walking around describing their live's with sentences that begin with phrases like: "What if, If only I would have, I wish I could do it over." You see, the hard knocks got the best of those people. Instead of being polished by the hard knocks of life and turning into a shining stone, they got beat up and bruised. When things got really tough, they didn't have principles they believed in enough to guide them through the tough times.

Let the hard knocks of life polish you and teach you lessons. Face life with principles and goals and you'll welcome the hardest of knocks with unshakeable confidence in yourself. In this way, you will discover who you really are, what you are really made of, and what you have the power to become. Believe in what you are working toward and go for it until you get it. Today might be your last chance to be all that you can be. And as you pursue your happiness, pray the "Fisherman's Prayer:"

"Fisherman's Prayer"

I pray that I may live to fish until my dying day.
And when it comes to my last cast, I then most humbly pray,
When in the Lord's great landing net and peacefully asleep,
That in His mercy
I be judged
BIG ENOUGH TO KEEP!!

235